EDGAR'S WALKING
GUIDES

JACK THE RIPPER'S EAST END

Copyright © Edgar's Guides Ltd, 2020

All rights reserved. No part of this book may be reprinted or reproduced or utilised in any form or by any electronic, mechanical or other means, now known or hereafter invented, including photocopying and recording, or in any information storage or retrieval system, without the prior permission in writing of the publishers.

All images publisher's own unless stated. Contemporary newspaper illustrations courtesy the British Library Board.

ISBN 978-1-8382342-0-1

Published by Edgar's Guides Ltd
71-75 Shelton Street, London WC2H 9JQ

Peruse the full catalogue,
access video clips and download free extras at
www.EdgarsGuides.com

No. 1

JACK THE RIPPER'S EAST END

EDGAR SAYS

"There's something utterly thrilling about conducting one's own tour of history as you perambulate the thoroughfares, away from the crowds, able to pause on a whim to savour the moment. Allow me to be your companion as I guide you to some of my favourite places, from the well-known to the obscure, and suggest some of my preferred establishments for refreshment along the way. My thanks to my chums Mr. Richard Jones and Mr. Adam Wood for mapping out this excursion."

SAFETY NOTICE

Please be sure to be careful as you walk the route. Stay familiar with your surroundings at all times, and take particular care when you are crossing roads. Every effort has been made to ensure that the directions are accurate, but obviously, things can change and mistakes can be made, so the publishers cannot be held responsible for errors or their consequences. In the current Covid-aware times there are sanitising pots at Underground stations, which we recommend using before setting out. Please also be aware that some parts of the route may require the wearing of face masks, so ensure you have one with you at all times. Other than that, enjoy the walk and I hope it brings you as much joy as it did me when I encountered the wonderful places that you will be visiting.

JACK THE RIPPER'S EAST END

Start: Aldgate East Underground Station, Exit 1 (Junction of Leman Street and Whitechapel High Street)

End: The Ten Bells public house
84 Commercial Street E1 6LY

Duration: 3 hours 45 minutes

Best of Times: Any time, but note some stops close at dusk. If you are planning on paying your respects at the grave sites, please note that gates close late afternoon.

The Jack the Ripper murders occurred over a period of twelve weeks (between 31st August and 9th November) in the autumn of 1888. During this period five women – Mary Ann Nichols, Annie Chapman, Elizabeth Stride, Catherine Eddowes and Mary Kelly – were found dead in Whitechapel, Spitalfields and the City of London, with their throats cut and, with the exception of Elizabeth Stride, their bodies horrifically mutilated.

At first the killer was referred to as the Whitechapel murderer, or fiend, then 'Leather Apron'. But then, in late September, 1888, a letter was sent to a London news agency which purported to come from the killer, and which boasted how the police couldn't catch him and that he wanted to get to work again. The letter was signed 'Jack the Ripper' – a name that chillingly and perfectly encapsulated the horror and revulsion that people were feeling about the crimes. Perhaps foolishly, the Metropolitan Police decided to publish the letter in the national press, with the result that the moniker caught on immediately and hundreds of hoax letters were sent in under the signature of what would, ever after, be the name by which the unknown killer would be known.

However, the Jack the Ripper murders are part of a more extensive police file under the wider title of the Whitechapel Murders, and this contains the details of eleven murder victims, ranging chronology-wise from Tuesday, 3rd April 1888, when Emma Elizabeth Smith was fatally attacked, to Friday, 13th February 1891, when Frances Coles was murdered.

Because Jack the Ripper was never caught, we don't really know, for sure, how many of these eleven women were his victims, and therefore any serious student of the case should acquaint themselves with the facts behind all eleven murders.

And that's where this little book comes in. In the course of this tour you will visit all but one of the Whitechapel Murders sites, and be able to conduct your own on-the-ground investigation into each of the crimes.

But you will also visit many other places connected with the story that people rarely see, from the decaying remains of the mortuary to which the bodies of several of the victims were taken, to the police station where many of the officers were based who were tasked with bringing the murderer to justice and ending his reign during the so-called Autumn of Terror.

You will walk through hidden streets that have changed little, if at all, since the days when those involved in the case lived in or walked along them. You will stop off at pubs where the victims drank, gaze upon churches, inside which some of them worshipped, and stroll down narrow cobbled alleyways that are still so sinister that it would come as no great surprise if some nefarious Victorian character, or even Jack the Ripper himself, were to spring from the shadows intent on who knows what. To that end, you will also see several locations connected to some of the many suspects whose names have, over the years, been put forward for the mantle of the most infamous serial killer of all time.

This is an historical guide to *all* the Whitechapel murders, so, step by step, you will be taken through the story as it unfolded between 1888 and 1891. You will be presented with the facts about the events that occurred at each and every site. In addition – and this is what makes this such a unique experience – your exploration will be enhanced by original photographs of the sites that you will be visiting, thus enabling you to gaze upon the scenes as they are today whilst also viewing them as they were at the time of the shocking events that took place there.

The tour can be done, at a fairly relaxed pace, in around three to four hours, although it is a self-guided tour and, since you set the pace, you can do it in a way that proves most comfortable for you, even doing it in sections over several days should you so desire. You can stop off at places that attract your interest; linger at spots that you wish to linger at for as long as your group wants to, and even partake of the hospitality of the many East End pubs you will be passing, where you can enjoy a pint, or two, and discuss and debate the case with your friends and family.

The book you are holding in your hands serves as your very own time machine that will transport you back to 1888, and enable you and your group to conduct your very own CSI and discover the full story and facts behind Victorian London's greatest mystery.

And, thanks to the detailed directions, I will be with you every step of the way, ensuring that you get to see as much as it is possible to see, ensuring that you don't take a wrong turn, telling you the story and the facts.

And ensuring that, by the time you sit down to enjoy your well-earned pint in the Ten Bells pub at the end of the tour, you will be a fully-fledged Ripperologist with an unrivalled understanding of the history, the facts, and the East End streets – not to mention one or two of the local hostelries.

The mystery awaits you – let the adventure begin!

Edgar's Guide To...

HIGHLIGHTS OF THE JACK THE RIPPER'S EAST END WALK

Here are some of the highlights you will encounter as you make your way through the thoroughfares of Whitechapel, Spitalfields and Aldgate in the footsteps of the world's most notorious serial killer:

- The sites of ten Whitechapel murders, and the cemeteries in which the victims are buried.
- The soaring tower of the church that dominates its surroundings today, just as it did in 1888, and upon which every one of Jack the Ripper's victims would have looked at on an almost daily basis.
- The sinister arch through which the possible first victim of Jack the Ripper passed, with a man whose evil intent she was unaware of.
- The crumbling remnants of the mortuary to which the bodies of several victims were taken.
- The police station where several of the officers who investigated the case were based.
- The doorway in which an infamous message was found scrawled in chalk on the wall.

- The Ten Bells pub, where several of the victims may have drunk, possibly even under the steely gaze of the Ripper himself.
- The buildings in which the inquests into the deaths of several victims were held.
- Old and historic streets, lined by 19th century houses, which as you walk along will convince you that you have somehow been transported back to that long ago era of gaslight and shadow when the spectre-like Jack the Ripper prowled the East End.

To begin, turn right out of Aldgate East Underground Station and cross Leman Street via the pedestrian crossing. Keep ahead along the flagstone path to the right of the grassed area, and pass the Clayton Hotel. On arrival at the traffic lights, use them to cross over Commercial Road, veer right on the other side and then turn first left into Manningtree Street, at the end of which turn left along Whitechurch Lane. Cross to its right side, and then pause on the corner just past the red phone box, to the right of which is the red-brick St Mary's Clergy House. Note the public drinking fountain, which dates from 1860 and is visible on the bottom-right in the photograph opposite. Behind the fountain is the site of

1. ST MARY'S CHURCH

Originally built in the Middle Ages, the church of St Mary Matfelon, popularly known as St Mary's

Whitechapel, was originally a limewashed building that became a striking local landmark which gained the nickname of 'the White Chapel'. In time, this name would pass to the district that grew up around the church. It was rebuilt in 1877 but burnt down three years later and, having been rebuilt once again, was re-opened in 1882. The church was destroyed by bombing in the Second World War, although fragments of it can still be seen scattered around the park ahead of you.

In the early hours of the morning of Tuesday, 3rd April 1888 Emma Elizabeth Smith, a 45-year-old widow, was walking along Whitechapel Road, when, as she passed the railings of the church, she noticed a group of youths coming towards her. Something about them appears to have made her uneasy, and she hurried across Whitechapel Road hoping to avoid them.

Cross Whitechapel Road via the traffic lights, veer left on the other side and then pause on the corner to look up

2. OSBORN STREET

The corner where you are now standing is where

Ripper victim Mary Ann 'Polly' Nichols, of whom we shall hear much more later, was last alive by anyone other than her killer. She had been thrown out of her usual lodging house, Wilmott's on Thrawl Street, because she did not have the fourpence needed for a bed, so wandered the streets looking to earn the money in the only way she knew how. At 2.30am she met her roommate at Wilmott's, Ellen Holland, here on the corner of Osborn Street and Whitechapel High Street. Polly was drunk and was leaning against a wall,

The corner of Osborn Street and Whitechapel High Street, indicated by a white star, was where Mary Ann Nichols was last seen alive – and where you are standing right now

She bragged that she'd made her doss money three times over, but had already drunk it away. Ellen tried to convince her to come back to the lodging house with her, but Polly refused. She was set on earning the money for her bed, claiming that she would simply find a man to share a bed with. Ellen watched Polly weave her way along Whitechapel Road. She was found murdered just over an hour later.

Look up Osborn Street and compare it with the photograph above, which shows how the street would have looked as a terrified Emma Smith hurried along it heading for her lodgings, with the men she had noticed by the railings of St Mary's now following her. Emma no doubt picked up her pace, but the men caught up with her as she reached the junction with Wentworth Street, a little further up on the left, as indicated on the photo by the black star. By what was the site of the Taylor Brothers Cocoa and Mustard Factory she was beaten and robbed, suffering terrible injuries. She somehow managed to stagger to the lodging house on nearby George Street where she had lived for 18 months. Here, the deputy keeper, Mary Russell, was so concerned by the state she was in that she immediately took her to the London Hospital, where she was examined by House Surgeon Dr. George Haslip, who noted that her head was bruised and her right ear torn, in addition to a ruptured peritoneum and internal organs. Emma survived for just over 24 hours, passing away at nine o'clock on the morning of 4th April 1888. Her attack is the first entry in the Metropolitan Police's Whitechapel murders file.

Cross over Osborn Street and continue along Whitechapel High Street, passing the Whitechapel Art Gallery. Pause outside the KFC to view the narrow white-painted building immediately to its left. Although rebuilt in 1900, this was formerly

3. YE OLDE ANGEL INN

Martha Tabram, believed by some to have been the first victim of Jack the Ripper, had been out drinking with her friend Mary Ann Connolly – better known as 'Pearly Poll' – on the evening of 6th August 1888. At some stage the pair met two soldiers in the Two Brewers public house on Brick Lane. Over the course of the evening the foursome visited several pubs, making their way down to Whitechapel High Street, and it is likely that they drank in this pub amongst others.

 Between the Angel and KFC, squeeze into the narrow

4. ANGEL ALLEY

At 11.45pm the foursome paired off, no doubt for the women to pay in kind for their evening's drinks, with Pearly Poll escorting her partner, a Corporal, up Angel Alley, where you are now standing. In 1888 Angel Alley was much longer, but today you can only go as far as the locked gate a little way along it. The alley has been home to the Freedom Press, Britain's oldest anarchist publisher, for fifty years.

Ye Olde Angel Inn, marked with a black star, alongside which is the narrow Angel Alley, indicated by a white star.

☞ Backtrack out of Angel Alley and go right along Whitechapel High Street for a few moments, and then turn right immediately before the White Hart pub into Gunthorpe Street, which in 1888 was

---

5. GEORGE YARD

Although alterations were made to the pub in 1938 and again in 1969, much of what you see today would be familiar to 19th century residents, including the tripartite windows that look out onto Whitechapel High Street which could be, and still are, opened to serve people who either preferred to drink outside or had to, on account of their appearance.

A blue board on the pub's wall on the left a little way along Gunthorpe Street poses the question, "Who Was Jack The Ripper?" The board then goes on to discuss Ripper suspect George Chapman, who worked as a barber in the pub's cellar in 1890.

A little further along Gunthorpe Street, on the left, you will find a block of flats with the year '1886' emblazoned on the upper level. In 1888, this was Sir George's Home for Respectable Girls, part of the George Yard Mission that had been established here in 1856 by provisions merchant-turned evangelist George Holland.

On 27th September 1888 the *Daily News* published the following article, which illustrates the impact the Whitechapel murders had on local girls:

"Mr. George Holland, whose remarkable work has been going on for so very many years in premises occupying an obscure position in George Yard, Whitechapel, says that the sensation has affected his institution very greatly. He has some hundreds of young women connected with his place, and many of them have been afraid to stir out after dark. He is under some anxiety, too, lest ladies who have been wont to come down there on winter evenings to teach and entertain his young people, should be deterred by this latest addition to the evil reputation of Whitechapel."

The entrance to George Yard Buildings in 1938

> *Continue along Gunthorpe Street. According to the East London Advertiser, George Yard was "one of the most dangerous streets in the locality," but, for a seasoned street walker like Martha Tabram, it offered a reasonable amount of privacy for quick sex acts which were known as 'four-penny knee-tremblers'. Pause at the block of flats at the top on the left. This is the site of*

6. GEORGE YARD BUILDINGS

George Yard Buildings was occupied by tenants whom the *East London Observer* described, somewhat unflatteringly, as "people of the poorest description." Once its staircase lights had been extinguished at 11.00pm, the landings were cast into an impenetrable darkness that made them ideal for use by prostitutes and their clients. Martha would no doubt have been aware of this tucked-away spot, and it was for one of the building's dark and secluded landings that she headed to in the company of the soldier she had paired off with following their evening in the pubs nearby, or possibly even a later client.

We know nothing more about her until, a little after 5.00am, John Saunders Reeves, a waterside-labourer, left his rooms in George Yard Buildings and came down the stairs and discovered the body of Martha Tabram. Earlier, another tenant named Alfred Crow had seen her lying on the landing, but in the gloom he had assumed she was merely sleeping. As it was now getting light, Reeves was able to see that the woman was lying on her back in a pool of blood.

He hurried off to find a policeman and returned with Constable Thomas Barrett, whom he had encountered patrolling Wentworth Street. Three hours earlier PC Barrett had been on the same beat when he came across a soldier loitering near the entrance to George Yard, who told the officer he was "waiting for a chum who had gone with a girl." Barrett sent Reeves to fetch the nearest medic, Dr Timothy Killeen, who, having carried out an examination of the woman, pronounced life extinct and gave his opinion that she had been brutally murdered.

The attack on Martha Tabram had certainly been a frenzied one. Thirty-nine stab wounds pepper-potted her body from her throat to her lower abdomen. Dr Killeen later told the inquest that, in his opinion, the killer had used two different blades, the majority of the wounds having been inflicted with an ordinary pocket knife, whilst a deep wound to her breast had been dealt by "...some long, strong instrument [which could have been] a sword, bayonet or dagger..."

Today, there is a great deal of debate over whether Martha was a victim of Jack the Ripper, and therefore his first victim. Some commentators say she was not, because she had been *stabbed* as opposed to having her throat cut before her body was mutilated – injuries suffered by almost all the five 'canonical victims'. Others point out that her killer targeted her throat and lower abdomen, just as Jack the Ripper would do with the later victims, and this may be an indication of a serial killer 'learning his trade'. Either way, Martha's death set people thinking that something untoward was happening in Whitechapel, and a general feeling of extreme unease began to ripple through the district. And when, just a few weeks later, another murder occurred, that unease gave way to outright terror and panic.

Make your way to the top of Gunthorpe Street, turn left along Wentworth Street, and go over the black-and-white Zebra crossing to pause before the red-brick arch dated 1886. The date commemorates the opening of Rothschilds Buildings, a large block of 'model dwellings' designed to house the poor. Situated on nearby Thrawl Street, the Buildings were demolished between 1973 and 1980, and this arch – formerly the entrance to the dwellings – moved to its present site.

Backtrack past the Zebra crossing, keeping to the left side of Wentworth Street, and pause at its junction with Brick Lane. The office building on the left corner plot stands on the site of the Taylor Brother's Cocoa and Mustard Factory, by which Emma Smith was fatally attacked. Go left along Brick Lane and pause at the next turning on the left, by the NHS health centre. The building in front of you is

....

7. THE FORMER FRYING PAN PUBLIC HOUSE

In 1888, Thrawl Street, on the corner of which the Frying Pan stands, was, according to the *East London Observer*, "one of the most unpromising places which can be found in this vast metropolis. Here, filth and squalor and wretchedness appear on every hand; cleanliness has no home within its confines…" It was lined with common lodging houses, the last refuge before the street or the workhouse for the destitute poor of the district. At these establishments men and women paid fourpence for a single bed or eightpence for a double bed, and they slept in dormitories or cubicles.

Life for the residents was a daily battle for survival, and many would dull the pain of their everyday existences by drinking in the many pubs nearby. The

'Singles' and 'Doubles' in a common lodging house, 1886

Frying Pan was one such pub. Indeed, if you look up at the red brick gable, you will see two crossed frying pans, and its original name emblazoned above them.

Residing at a lodging house at 18 Thrawl Street for the three weeks prior to 30th August 1888 was a lady whom the other residents knew simply as 'Polly', although today we know that her actual name was Mary Ann Nichols.

So far as we know, she had been drinking in the Frying Pan until 12.30am early on the morning of 31st August. She had then made her way back to the lodging house, where the deputy keeper refused her admittance because she didn't have the fourpence for her bed. She was wearing a bonnet that no-one had seen her with before, and, as she walked away,

Edgar's Guide To...

The Frying Pan public house on the corner of Thrawl Street

apparently intending to resort to prostitution to raise the money for her accommodation, she turned back to the deputy keeper and jauntily predicted: "I'll soon get my doss money; see what a jolly bonnet I've got now," evidently confident that this headgear would prove an irresistible draw to potential clients. We will pick up Polly's story later on our tour.

Continue along Brick Lane, go over Fashion Street and keep ahead along Brick Lane. Be sure to admire the now-disused fountain (dated 1860) on the left in front of Christ Church Primary School. Go next left into Fournier Street and pause on the corner to look over at the

8. BRICK LANE JAMME MASJID OR BRICK LANE MOSQUE

This building really does reflect the changing demographics of the East End of London. It was built in 1743 as a chapel for the Huguenots, who had arrived in the district in ever-increasing numbers throughout the first half of the 18th century. The year '1743' can be seen on the sundial that adorns the building's upper level, as well as the sobering motto *Umbra Sumus* ("We Are But Shadows"). In 1809 it was purchased by the London Society for Propagating Christianity among the Jews, and ten years later it became a Methodist chapel. In the 1880s, the district around the chapel saw a huge influx of migrants fleeing persecution in Eastern Europe and so, in 1897, the building became a synagogue. In turn, in the 1970s the Jewish population began to move out of the area, to be replaced by a vibrant Bangladeshi community, and thus, in 1976, the building became a mosque.

Continue along the right side of Fournier Street, a truly enchanting enclave along which the houses

on either side were constructed by and for Huguenot refugees in the 1720s. They were skilled silk weavers, and these sturdy houses were built as homes and workshops. The weaving took place in the attics, where you can still see the airy windows designed to admit as much light as possible to work by. It was in Fournier Street that the fabric for Queen Victoria's wedding dress was woven. She chose to break with the norm by wearing a white dress, and in consequence the fashion for white weddings is said to have begun. By the 1880s, however, the silk weavers had moved on, and these houses were lived in by the burgeoning Jewish population of the district. Three-quarters of the way along Fournier Street turn right into Wilkes Street, again lined, largely, by 18th century houses. Be sure to look right along Princelet Street as you pass it, another true survivor of the bygone East End, and ponder the thought that many of the houses you have been and are passing were here in 1888. At the end of Wilkes Street turn right into Hanbury Street, cross to its left side, and pause outside the large white '29' on the windows on the left a little way along.

....

9. 29 HANBURY STREET

In 1888 the property consisted of eight rooms, in which seventeen people lived. In appearance it was

29 Hanbury Street: scene of the murder of Annie Chapman

similar to the buildings which survive today behind you on the south side of Hanbury Street. No. 29 was the site of the murder of Annie Chapman. Early in the morning of Saturday, 8th September 1888, 56-year-old John Davis went downstairs from his room on the third floor. As he stepped into the ground-floor hallway he noticed that the front door, which lead out onto Hanbury Street, was wide open. Mr. Davis thought nothing of it, as in the two weeks he and his family had taken lodgings there he had never known the door to be locked. Davis turned toward the back door and the yard beyond, where the outside privy was situated. As he pushed the door open and started down the few steps, to his left he saw the body of a woman lying between the steps and the fence separating the yard to that of No. 27. The official Metropolitan Police report records the discovery as follows:

"...a woman lying on her back, dead, left arm resting on left breast, legs drawn up, abducted, small intestines and flap of the abdomen lying on right side, above right shoulder attached by a cord with the rest of the intestines inside the body; two flaps of skin from the lower part of the abdomen lying in a large quantity of blood above the left shoulder; throat cut deeply from left and back in a jagged manner right around the throat."

After first alerting three workers in Hanbury Street,

The rear yard of 29 Hanbury Street. Annie Chapman's body was found between the fence and the rear steps

Davis went to inform the police. Inspector Joseph Chandler, examining the yard, found six spots of blood where the head had lain 18 inches up the wall of the house, ranging in size from a sixpence down to a point. On the fence dividing No. 29 from No. 27 he found "smears of blood" about 14 inches from the ground. Apart from this, no clues were found.

In the early 1900s Nathaniel Brill opened a barber's shop in the front of No. 29, operating for almost fifty years. After he closed up the ground floor remained empty, although other parts of the house were occupied until the north side of Hanbury Street was demolished in March 1970 as the Truman Brewery was extended, and since 2004 has been part of a vibrant market site.

Continue along Hanbury Street, cross over Brick Lane and keep ahead along the continuation of Hanbury Street, keeping to its right side and taking your time to admire the street art that adorns this stretch of road. Keep ahead over Spelman Street, then cross Hanbury Street to go left along Daplyn Street. Hobson's Place, the block of flats to your right, stands on the site of Pelham Street, which in the 1880s was the home of

10. ROSE MYLETT'S MOTHER

There were fears that the Ripper had resumed his grim work in the early hours of 20th December 1888, when the body of a young woman was found in a yard in Poplar, three miles from Whitechapel. The unknown victim was examined by Dr. George Harris, who noted that the lips were livid and the mouth was closed; blood-flecked mucus issued from the nostrils, and the hands were half-clenched. The body was removed to the Bickmore Street mortuary, where her clothing was searched and the body examined.

She would soon be identified; her name was Catherine Mylett, known sometimes as 'Rose', and her mother lived here in Pelham Street. A newspaper report described the heartbreaking moment when police officers arrived to break the tragic news:

"When the detectives called at the house on Boxing Day they found the inmates indulging in Christmas festivities, and upon stating the object of their visit one of the women in the house had a serious fit."

Rose herself had lived at 18 George Street, the same common lodging house as early victim Emma Smith, and it is a mystery why she had been at Poplar where she met her end. The inquest into her death concluded that she had been murdered by strangulation, but there were no other injuries and the police attempted to get the decision overturned to one of 'Death by natural causes'.

Continue along Daplyn Street to turn right along Woodseer Street, where a true surprise awaits you. On the left you will see a line of tiny cottages, which are

11. ALBERT COTTAGES

These tiny and picturesque houses were built in the 1850s by the Metropolitan Association for Improving the Dwellings of the Industrial Classes, to provide homes for small artisan families who could not afford the higher rents charged by the larger family units that London's philanthropic bodies were then erecting in the poorer parts of the Victorian metropolis. They were originally divided into two units, an upstairs and a downstairs, each of which would accommodate one family. They really do evoke a sense of the old East End, and it is well worth taking your time to admire them. In particular, be sure to look through the arched iron gate you can see behind Albert Cottages, at the lovely little gardens in front of each house. The cottages were initially frowned upon, as the fashion at the time favoured large blocks that could accommodate lots of families, but they now provide us with a true insight into the cottage accommodation that was once common but is now quite rare in the East End.

....

Continue along Woodseer Street, and pause to look over at Victoria Cottages, built in 1865, effectively duplicates of Albert Cottages, and again the gardens behind the house are well worth taking a look at. Turn right along Deal Street, cross to its left side, and at its end go left along Hanbury Street and follow it until you reach the 'Give Way' sign at its end. This is the approximate spot where PC Jonas Mizen was approached by Charles Cross and Robert Paul, about whom you will learn much more very shortly, so be patient my eager sleuths. Cross Vallance Road via the pedestrian crossing, and veer right to cross Wodeham Gardens and pass the line of shops. Take the next left into Durward Street, keeping to its left side. Go over Castlemaine Street and pause by the Sports Centre to look ahead at the large brick building, which is

12. THE FORMER BOARD SCHOOL

At around 3.40am on 31st August 1888 a carter named Charles Cross was making his way to work along the section of Buck's Row – as Durward Street was then known – to the left of the looming bulk of the red-brick building in front of you. It is now flats, but it was formerly a Board School that had been built in 1876. The children used to play on the roof of the building, hence the railings that still enclose the space. Cross was heading from the opposite direction, coming toward the school, when he noticed a dark bundle lying in the gateway of some stables that then stood to the left of and behind the school building.

Like so many of the district's alleyways and

Buck's Row in 1938, with the Board School on the right. Mary Ann Nichols' body was found at the spot marked with a white star.

passageways in the area, street lighting in Buck's Row was minimal, and, at first, Cross could not be sure what exactly the bundle was. It looked something like a discarded tarpaulin, so, thinking that it might prove useful for his job as a carter or delivery driver, he went to inspect it and discovered to his horror that it was, in fact, the prone body of a woman, who proved to be Mary Ann Nichols.

As Cross stood, rooted to the spot and unsure of what to do next, he heard footsteps behind him. Turning, he saw another carter, Robert Paul, walking towards him. "Come and look over here," Cross called, "there is a woman lying on the pavement."

The two crossed and stooped down over her. She was lying on her back, her legs straight out, and her skirts were raised almost over her waist. Charles Cross reached out and touched her face, which was warm, and her hands, which were cold and limp. "I believe she is dead," he observed. Robert Paul, meanwhile, placed his hand on the woman's chest, and thought he felt a slight movement. "I think she's breathing," he said, "but very little if she is." Paul suggested that they sit the woman up, but Cross refused to touch her again.

Deciding – perhaps somewhat callously – that they were late for work and had done as much as they could, they pulled her skirts back down to her knees to preserve her decency, and set off for their respective places of employment, agreeing to tell the first policeman they encountered of their find.

But what neither man had noticed in the pitch darkness of Buck's Row was that the woman's throat had been slashed so savagely that her head had almost been cut from her body.

That discovery was made by beat officer Police Constable John Neil, who turned into Buck's Row and proceeded to walk past the Board School shortly after Cross and Paul had left the scene. "There was not a soul about," he later told the inquest. "I had been round there half an hour previously, and saw no-one then. I was on the right side... when I noticed a figure lying in the street. It was dark at the time... I examined the body by the aid of my lamp, and noticed blood oozing from a wound in the throat. She was lying on her back, with her clothes disarranged. I felt her arm, which was quite warm from the joints upwards. Her eyes were wide open. Her bonnet was off and lying at her side."

As Neil stooped down over the body, he noticed PC John Thain passing the end of the street and flashed his lantern to attract his attention. "Here's a woman with her throat cut," he called to his approaching colleague. "Run at once for Dr Llewellyn."

As Thain hurried off to fetch the medic, PC Mizen, who had been alerted by Cross and Paul, arrived at the scene. Neil sent him to bring reinforcements, and asked him to fetch the police ambulance.

When Dr Llewellyn arrived, at around 4.00am, he carried out a cursory examination of the body and, noting the severity of the wounds to the throat, pronounced life extinct. On closer examination he also observed that the deceased's body and legs were still warm, although her hands and wrists were quite cold. This led him to surmise that she could not have been dead for more than half an hour.

As Llewellyn went about his grim business, news of the murder was beginning to filter through the immediate neighbourhood and people began arriving at the scene. Alarmed by these sightseers, the doctor ordered the police to take her to the mortuary where he would make a more detailed examination. Thus the body was placed on a police ambulance, which was little more than a wheelbarrow, and was taken to the Whitechapel Workhouse mortuary.

Inspector Spratling arrived at 5.30am to take down a description of the deceased. At first he noticed only the neck wounds previously noted by Dr Llewellyn, but on closer inspection he discovered something that had so far eluded everyone. Beneath her bloodstained clothing a deep gash ran all the way along the woman's abdomen; she had been disembowelled. Jack the Ripper's reign of terror had begun.

Walk past the Board School, pausing to take in the small area to the left of the new entrance to Whitechapel Underground station - this is the approximate spot where Mary Ann Nichols was murdered. Resume walking along Durward Street. You are now heading in the direction from which Charles Cross approached the murder site. Continue all the way

Edgar's Guide To...

The Working Lads' Institute

to the end then turn right into Brady Street, with the red bricked buildings on your right. (On the other side of the road is Sainsbury's, with public toilets should you be in need of a comfort break!). At the end of Brady Street, turn right onto Whitechapel Road. Continue for a few minutes, then almost immediately as you reach Budgens on your right pause outside the soaring redbrick exterior of

---

13. THE WORKING LADS' INSTITUTE

Built in 1884/85 and opened by Alexandra, Princess of Wales, on 31st October 1885 with her husband, the future Edward VII, in attendance. It was built as a philanthropic facility promoting the welfare of local employed young men aged thirteen and over, offering evening education and exercise. Facilities included dormitories, classrooms, a lecture room, and a reading room named the Alexandra Room overlooking the street, and it was here that the inquests into the deaths of several victims of Jack the Ripper were held.

Deputy Coroner George Collier held the inquiry into the death of Martha Tabram here on 9th and 23rd August 1888. Coroner Wynne Edwin Baxter presided over the four-day inquest into the death of Mary Ann Nichols here, as well as the inquest into Annie Chapman's death over five days beginning on

10th September, thereby overseeing the Nichols and Chapman inquests simultaneously.

Baxter's decision to move inquests from the usual pub function room was well received, and the *East London Advertiser* of 15th September 1888 commented:

"A word may be said as to the great advantage there is in selecting such a place as the Lads' Institute for coroner's inquiries. The hall is lofty and light, while there is plenty of room for everyone."

The inquests on later victims Alice McKenzie and Frances Coles were also held here.

The Working Lads' Institute morphed into the Whitechapel Primitive Methodist Mission, providing "a home for friendless and orphan lads." The Mission moved to new premises nearby in 1906, and this building operated as a hostel for young men aged between 17 and 21, and was sold in 1971. The upper floors were converted into nine flats in 1997.

Resume walking along Whitechapel Road, and after a few steps note the building now housing the pawnbrokers and Paddy Power betting shop which was once the Grave Maurice pub, a favourite of the Kray twins. Note the wording set out on the cream panel between the two rows of upper windows. It was at pubs such as this that inquests were often held in the days before Coroners' Courts were established. As you continue note the large black gas lamp bracket above you on your right, with the narrow doorways to Woods Buildings almost beneath - an open alleyway in 1888, and quite likely the route by which the murderer escaped after killing Mary Ann Nichols - and pause by the drinking fountain on your left, upon which a black statue of an angel stands.

14. THE EDWARD VII FOUNTAIN

This vantage point affords several views of interest. The fountain itself, by the sculptor W.S. Frith, was erected in 1911 in memory of King Edward VII, paid for by the subscription of local Jewish businessmen, at a time when it was common for drinking fountains to be made available to quench the public's thirst, given that a piped water supply was a rarity and the main alternative was the pub. Take particular note of the cherubs that sit around the corners, and which hold representations of the high-tech of the age, such as a car and a ship.

Among the row of shops behind you is the Ukay International Saree Centre; this was the dingy venue where Joseph Merrick, the Elephant Man, was exhibited by his manager Tom Norman upon his arrival in London from Leicester in November 1884.

Although Joseph visited Dr Frederick Treves at the London Hospital, opposite, at this time, it was not until 1886 that he took up permanent residence there in a set of secluded rooms known as 'Bedstead Square'. The same shop was the venue two years later, during the height of the Ripper scare, of a temporary display of wax depictions of the victims comprising crudely-made life-sized figures with red paint liberally splashed around, viewable after paying an entrance fee.

☞ *Resume walking along Whitechapel Road. On reaching Court Street on your right, cross over and pause by the mounted Underground roundel on the black plinth and look over Whitechapel Road, slightly to your left, to take in*

15. THE ROYAL LONDON HOSPITAL

The Royal London was founded in September 1740 as the London Infirmary, changing its name to the London Hospital in 1748. The hospital façade dates from 1757, but is not now in use for medical practice; new facilities were opened in the extensive grounds behind the frontage in 2012. At the time of writing, the original buildings are currently being converted for use as the Tower Hamlets Civic Centre.

The London Hospital itself has several links to the Whitechapel murders. It was here that Emma Smith, having been treated by Dr George Haslip, died from her injuries. The inquest into her death was also held here, presided over by Coroner Wynne Baxter.

James Sadler, who was arrested for the murder of possible Ripper victim Frances Coles, was treated here for injuries he sustained in a mugging on the night of her death. Ripper suspect Robert Donston Stephenson, who was treated at the Hospital between July and December 1888, told a fellow patient that the actions of a surgeon there, Dr Morgan Davies, were suspicious; the patient, George Marsh, considered Stephenson more curious still and reported his suspicions to Scotland Yard.

Cross over Whitechapel Road via the traffic lights, towards the London Hospital, and on the other side turn right. Go past the red phone box and the bicycle racks, and then left into Turner Street. Keep ahead, passing the Dental Hospital on the left, and go straight on, cross over Stepney Way, and keep ahead along the continuation of Turner Street (the Good Samaritan pub will be to your right), passing the red-brick St Philip's church on your left. Turn left into Newark Street, with its evocative row of old houses that retain the feel of their 19th century origins. A little way along on the left, immediately before the 'No Entry' signs, is

....

16. THE ROYAL LONDON HOSPITAL MUSEUM

On the evening of 16th October, 1888, Mr George Lusk, President of the Mile End Vigilance Committee, received the infamous 'From Hell' letter, purporting to have been written by the murderer, and containing a portion of kidney which, so the letter claimed, the author "took from one victim" – the inference being that it was part of the kidney that had been removed from Catherine Eddowes, the Mitre Square victim, who we shall hear about soon.

Lusk's initial reaction was to dismiss it as the sick prank of a medical student and he presumed that the kidney was that of a sheep or some other animal. He did, however, seek the opinion of other members of the Committee, who considered that it might actually be genuine. They took the kidney to a local medic, who examined it and opined that it was a fragment of a human kidney, but suggested they get a second opinion, and it was duly brought here to the London Hospital, where Dr Thomas Openshaw, the Pathological Curator, examined it through a microscope and pronounced it to be half of a left

George Lusk and the 'From Hell' letter

Dr Thomas Openshaw
and the 'mikerscope' letter
he received

human kidney, although he also stated that he couldn't be sure if it had belonged to a man or a woman.

Several newspapers, however, wrote that Openshaw had confirmed that it was indeed part of the kidney that had been taken from Catherine Eddowes body, and, as a result, Openshaw became so alarmed by the inaccuracies that were appearing in various newspapers that he felt compelled to go on record in order to correct them. As a result of this press coverage, another Jack the Ripper letter writer decided to target Openshaw with his very own hoax missive:

"Old boss you was rite it was the left kidny i was goin to hoperate agin close to you ospitle just as i was going to dror mi nife along of er bloomin throte them cusses of coppers spoilt the game but i guess i wil be on the jobn soon and will send you another bit of innerds

Jack the Ripper

O have you seen the devle with his mikerscope and scalpul a-lookin at a kidney with a slide cocked up."

You can see a copy of this letter, along with several other original exhibits relating to the murder of Catherine Eddowes, amongst the fascinating medical exhibits inside the Museum, which also contains artefacts connected with another famous former resident of the Hospital, Joseph Merrick, the so-called 'Elephant Man'. Entry is free, but please note that the Museum is open on Fridays only.

On leaving the Museum, backtrack along Newark Street turn left along Turner Street. Keep ahead over Ashfield Street, then turn right into Walden Street – as you walk along it, contrast the Victorian cottages on your left with the modern office blocks on your right. Fixed to the wall of number 12, between the two upper windows, is an old fire insurance mark. Continue along Walden Street, with the skyscrapers of the City of London looming ahead in the distance. Cross over New Road via the Zebra crossing, veer right on its other side and swerve left into Fordham Street. Keep ahead over Myrdle Street; if it wasn't for the cars you could feel you've gone back to Victorian Whitechapel. At the end of Fordham Street, pause at its left junction with Settles Street. This purple-painted building is

17. THE FORMER BRICKLAYERS ARMS

Victim Elizabeth Stride was seen standing in this doorway with a respectably-dressed man just before eleven o'clock, a couple of hours before her death, on Saturday 29th September 1888. It was raining heavily, and the couple appeared reluctant to venture out onto the street. Two men named Best and Gardner were entering the pub at the same time, and teased the man about how he was cuddling and kissing Elizabeth, despite her being so poorly dressed, and said to her, "That's Leather Apron getting round you," referring to the early nickname for the Whitechapel murderer. The couple ran out into the street and out of earshot from the jibes, heading south towards the Commercial Road, and we now follow in their footsteps.

Turn left along Settles Street, at the end of which turn right into Commercial Road and pause a

little way along to look over at the street opposite, which is

....

18. BATTY STREET

In June 1887, the summer before the Whitechapel murders, 22-year-old Miriam Angel – who was six months pregnant – was found dead in her bed at No. 16 Batty Street, three-quarters of the way down the street on the right-hand side. When Miriam failed to meet her mother-in-law for breakfast as arranged, an investigation found that the door to her room was locked from the inside. When it was forced open Miriam was discovered, with an empty bottle of nitric acid on the bed. She had been poisoned. Underneath the bed was Israel Lipski, a young immigrant who lived in an upstairs room, who had acid burns inside his mouth from swallowing a small quantity of acid himself. Lipski was tried and, despite the evidence against him being flimsy, was found guilty and hanged. From that point the name 'Lipski' became a slur against Jewish people in the area, as was seen the following autumn during the Whitechapel murders.

Three doors further down Batty Street, at No. 22, during the Ripper scare of the following year, lived a Mrs. Kuer. The German landlady took in lodgers on a short-term basis and charged a small fee to do their

The scene of the murder of Miriam Angel in Batty Street following its rebuild in 1888

laundry. In October 1888 she was handed four shirts knotted in a bundle by one lodger. This was not untied at the time, but when Mrs Kuer did so a few days later she found that one was saturated with blood. The police were called, and the premises watched for the lodger's return. When he eventually made an appearance he was taken into custody for questioning, but released some time later without charge.

Continue along Commercial Road, crossing Greenfield Road, and then cross over Commercial Road at the traffic lights. Veer left on the other side and turn immediately right into Henriques Street, which in 1888 was named Berner Street. Walk past the 1903 Cookery and Laundry building on your right, and pause by the red-bricked Bernhard Baron House on the left. Opposite you is

19. THE SITE OF DUTFIELD'S YARD

Forty-five minutes after leaving the Bricklayer's Arms in Settles Street, Elizabeth Stride was seen with her companion by various people around the vicinity of Berner Street, including at 12.30am by PC William Smith, who was on his beat. At that moment they were standing on the spot you are now, outside what

Berner Street, with the cartwheel indicating the entrance to Dutfield's Yard

was the London Board School and opposite No. 40 Berner Street, which was home to the International Working Men's Educational Club, a society open to any working man of any nationality who was a supporter of the Socialist movement. It officially had 75 to 80 members, but it was the end of the Jewish holiday and that evening a meeting had taken place at which some 90 to 100 people had heard a lecture entitled 'Judaism and Socialism'.

At 12.45am Israel Schwartz was walking towards his home at Ellen Street, at the southern end of Berner Street, when he saw a woman he would later identify as Elizabeth standing in the gateway to Dutfield's Yard, between Nos. 40 and 42, with a man who at first tried to pull her into the street but then turned her round and pushed her to the floor. Alarmed, Schwartz crossed the road and at that point became aware of another man nearby, lighting his pipe. The attacker called out "Lipski" – Schwartz was uncertain whether the insult was aimed at himself or the man lighting his pipe, although the police were later of the opinion that it was meant as a warning to Schwartz, and he hurriedly continued on his journey. He noticed that the second man appeared to be following him so started running, but on reaching the railway arch saw that the man was no longer behind him. The two men had left Elizabeth Stride at the entrance to Dutfield's Yard, its gates open, with her assailant. It was close to 12.50am.

Ten minutes later Louis Diemschitz, the steward of the International Working Men's Educational Club, returned to 40 Berner Street with his pony and costermonger's barrow, having been out at work since 11 o'clock that morning. His intention was to deposit his goods at the Club before taking his pony to stables half a mile away off Cable Street.

As he approached he saw that both gates were open, with the yard itself pitch black. As he drove through the gates the pony shied to the left; Diemschitz peered down into the inky darkness, and could just make out a shape on the floor to his right. He prodded it with his whip, then climbed down from his seat and lit a match. The glow, faint as it was, was sufficient to illuminate a woman lying near the wall. The steward went at once into the Club and found his wife, telling her and other members that there was a woman lying in the yard, but he was unsure whether she was drunk or dead. Lighting a candle and returning to the yard, Diemschitz could now see there was blood.

Within a quarter of an hour the yard was filled with Club members and police officers. First to arrive, within five or six minutes of the discovery, was PC Henry Lamb, who had been on his beat along Commercial Road when he saw two Club members running towards him, calling out "Come on, there has been another murder." Arriving at the scene, PC Lamb lit his lamp and saw that the woman's throat was cut, although there were no mutilations. He put his hand upon her face and it felt slightly warm, yet on feeling her wrist could detect no pulse.

Although debate has raged ever since as to whether Elizabeth Stride was a victim of Jack the Ripper, there is no doubt that she was the first of what is known as the 'Double Event' – two murders in one night.

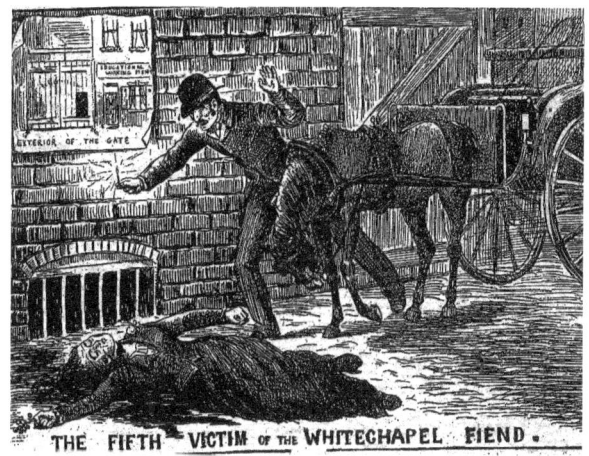

Louis Diemschitz discovers Elizabeth Stride in Dutfield's Yard

---

☞ *Continue walking down Henriques Street and turn right into Fairclough Street, then left onto Backchurch Lane. Note the old lifting devices and landing stages of the former warehouses as you pass along. Keep ahead past Boyd, Ellen and Hooper Streets, then left into Pinchin Street. Pause by the second arch on the right, the one with the square windows. This was the scene of the discovery of*

Pinchin Street in 1889

20. THE PINCHIN STREET TORSO

In the early hours of 10th September 1889 the body of a woman minus the head and legs was discovered in this arch by a constable who was on his beat along lonely Pinchin Street. There was no blood inside the arch itself, indicating that the victim had not died where the body was found, and dismemberment had taken place elsewhere. Medical examination suggested that death had occurred at least twenty-four hours before the discovery, so the trunk must have been kept in some place for a day or two before a decision was made where to dispose of it.

The remains were buried more than three weeks later, on 5th October, in a metal box filled with spirits to preserve the torso in order to assist in the possibility of matching it with the missing body parts should they be discovered. The strange coffin was soldered shut, then placed into a wooden box painted black and interred at the East London Cemetery, where they remain to this day, possibly perfectly preserved.

Continue walking along Pinchin Street, and at its end turn right and walk along Christian Street, where in 1888 a cigarette box maker named Leon Goldstein lived at No. 22. His shiny black work bag innocently caused alarm in the East End and became part of the myth of Jack the Ripper, who for evermore has been portrayed as carrying a shiny black case containing his medical instruments. Pass under the railway bridge, go left into Cable Street and cross over at the Zebra crossing, going left on the other side to keep going along Cable Street. It might seem that there is nothing here to interest you, but believe me, there is, so stick with it my dedicated sleuths. On arrival at the traffic lights pause for a moment to reflect on the fate of John Williams, who had been found guilty of the seven Ratcliffe Highway murders of 1811, but hunged himself in prison before he could be executed. As suicides could not be interred in consecrated ground, Williams' body was paraded through the streets followed by a crowd estimated at over 150,000 people to this crossroads, where he was buried – but not before a wooden stake had been driven through his heart to prevent his spirit from wandering. In 1886, a gas company excavating the road at this crossroads unearthed a skeleton, buried upside down and with the remains of a stake through its torso. It was reported that the landlord of the Crown and Dolphin kept the skull as a souvenir. Continue over Cannon Street Road, passing to the left of the Crown and Dolphin, and keep ahead along Cable Street. Be sure to admire the old Victorian cottages on the right as you pass. Just past the bus stop with the white 'B' on it, pause by the entrance to

21. ST GEORGE'S TOWN HALL

Built in 1860 and formerly known as the Vestry Hall, this was the setting for the inquest into the murder of Elizabeth Stride over five days in October 1888.

Presided over by Coroner Wynne Baxter, this was the first inquiry into the death of a Ripper victim not have been held at the Working Lads' Institute, and is notable for the strange story of Mrs Mary Malcolm, who appeared to testify that she had identified the body as being that of her sister, Elizabeth Watts; not from her facial features, but from a small black mark on a leg which was apparently the result of a snake bite in her youth.

Mrs Malcolm caused sensation when she claimed to have been visited by the spirit of her sister on the night of Elizabeth Stride's murder as she slept, distinctly feeling three kisses on her cheek. On reading that the 'visitation' had occurred at exactly the same time as the victim's death, Mrs Malcolm was convinced it was

The press report on Mary Malcolm's strange dream

her sister saying her last goodbye. At the inquest she went on to claim that her sister had led a less-than palatable lifestyle. The supernatural was discounted when her sister appeared in person to defend herself against the slur made against her character by Mrs Malcolm, who by now had disappeared.

In his summing up, Wynne Baxter pointed out that, despite the lack of abdominal mutilations, there were similarities to the previous murders of Mary Ann Nichols and Annie Chapman.

The inquest into the death Rose Mylett, and of the woman whose torso was found in the Pinchin Street arch, were also held here under Baxter.

 Backtrack past the bus stop and turn left through the gates. Immediately on the left is

22. A MURAL OF THE BATTLE OF CABLE STREET

On Sunday, 4th October 1936, members of the British Union of Fascists led by Oswald Mosley intended to march through the East End of London. An estimated 100,000 local residents signed a petition asking that the then-Home Secretary, John Simon, ban the march for fear it might erupt into violence.

He refused, and deployed a police escort to stop anti-fascist demonstrators disrupting the march.

The protesters blocked the route, whereupon the police moved in to disperse them. The demonstrators fought back, using sticks, rocks, bricks, chair legs and other improvised weapons. Local women hurled household rubbish, rotten vegetables and even the contents of chamber pots from the windows of their houses along Cable Street. Following several running battles Mosley agreed to abandon the march for fear of further serious bloodshed.

This colourful and detailed mural, depicting scenes from the battle, was painted between 1979 and 1983.

Walk ahead through the gates into St George's churchyard. When the path divides keep straight (ignoring the left path) and keep ahead to the ruined

23. ST GEORGE'S-IN-THE-EAST MORTUARY

Built in 1876, with an additional chamber added in 1890, this was the mortuary to which the body of Elizabeth Stride was taken and where the photograph of her in death was taken for identification purposes. It was also to here that the Pinchin Street torso was brought. It is a tiny building, and working inside it must have been both claustrophobic and unpleasant for the unfortunate doctors who had the unenviable task of conducting post mortems within its walls.

In 1904 it became a Nature museum, intended to teach the children of the district's slum dwellers about nature, something they rarely encountered in their daily lives. It appears to have been a popular attraction and, in the summer months, was visited by up to 1,000 people each day, most of them groups of local school children. The museum closed its doors in 1939, when many of the East End's children were evacuated at the outbreak of the Second World War.

The little building with its sad past is now boarded up, and becomes more and more derelict with every year that passes.

....

Head towards the church, keeping the gravestone-lined wall to your left; just before the gate note the tombstone with the skull and crossbones on it. Go through the gate of St George's Church. Head diagonally left across the flagstone court, pass through the gate, down the steps and turn right along The Highway. Keep ahead over Cannon Street Road and follow The Highway, turning right immediately after the Stranger's Rest Evangelical Church into Betts Street, and then left

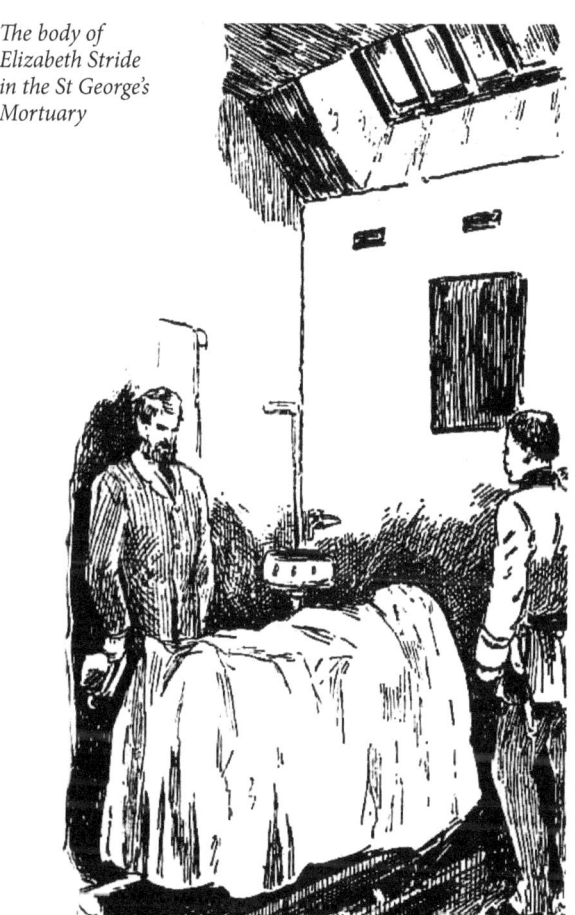

The body of Elizabeth Stride in the St George's Mortuary

through the gates, just before the Mary Sandbrook Day Nursery, into Swedenborg Gardens. Keep ahead along the flagstone path. At the end of the black railing to your right keep ahead, passing to the left of the Swedenborg Gardens board. On arrival at the rubbish bin, turn right up the steps and pause alongside the stone font of the former

24. SWEDISH CHURCH

Nothing but a few scattered stones and the font that you are standing by survive of this church, which was destroyed by bombing in the second World War. This was the first Swedish Church in London, erected here in 1728 by the Swedish author and mystic Emanuel Swedenborg, who lived in nearby Wellclose Square.

In 1888 the Clerk of the church was Sven Olsson. He appeared as a witness at the inquest into Elizabeth Stride's death, testifying that he had known her for seventeen years, and providing biographical details about her which he had gleaned from the register of the church at which she, as a Swedish woman by birth, used to worship.

Inspector Reid told the inquest that a Swedish Bible had been found at the deceased's lodgings, but Olsson corrected him, stating that it was, in fact, a hymn book

The Swedish Church

that he had given to her the previous winter.

👉 *With your back to the font, go down the small steps, at the bottom of which veer right past the tree, keeping the children's playground to your right. Keep straight towards the gate; go through it and turn right. Proceed through the three grey posts, follow the asphalt road as it veers left, and keep ahead, with St Paul's School to your left. Keep ahead and head into*

Graces Alley, where on the right is

....

25. WILTON'S MUSIC HALL

Built in the 1740s as an alehouse, it became known as The Mahogany Bar from the 1820s to reflect its dark wooden fixtures and fittings. A concert room was built behind the bar in 1839, and was greatly enlarged by new owner John Wilton who opened it in 1859 as a 1,500 capacity Music Hall where artists such as Arthur Lloyd, George Ware and 'Champagne Charlie' George Leybourne performed. It is believed to be the oldest surviving music hall in Europe.

Fire ravaged the building in 1877 and, following a period of repair lasting eight years, the property passed into the hands of the Methodist Church, who ran it as The Mahogany Bar Mission to help the area's destitute, including the installation of a soup kitchen in the bar in 1889.

It served as a rag warehouse in the 1950s, and escaped demolition plans during the slum clearances of the 1960s thanks to a campaign supported by the likes of Sir John Betjeman. It was awarded Grade II-listed status in 1971 and, after many years of restoration, reopened as a performance venue in 1997.

Today, Wiltons continues to stage theatre

productions, and has been used as a setting in many films, including *Interview With The Vampire*, and music videos such as Frankie Goes To Hollywood's *Relax*. The Mahogany Bar is open from Monday to Friday, 5.00-11.00pm, and is well worth a visit to explore this wonderful relic of a bygone era.

At the end of Graces Alley turn right onto Ensign Street, then left along Cable Street, where on the left is the Jack the Ripper Museum (currently accessible by appointment only: see www.jacktherippermuseum. com). Cross to the right side of Cable Street, and then cross over Leman Street via the traffic lights. Keep ahead along Royal Mint Street, keeping to its right side, and turn right, just after Enterprise Cars, to squeeze along the narrow and sinister path that snakes beneath the railway arch. You are now passing through an atmospheric, not to say sinister, little section that gives you some idea of what the murder site you are coming to would have appeared in 1891. When you exit into Chamber Street, turn left and cross to its right side, to pause by the lamppost immediately before the railway bridge. Opposite you is a coffee-coloured office frontage, which covers the entrance to the former

26. SWALLOW GARDENS

At 2.15am on 13th February 1891 PC Ernest Thompson, who had only joined the Metropolitan Police three months earlier and out on his first unsupervised beat, was walking along Chamber Street when he heard the sound of a man's footsteps retreating.

Seconds later he was here at Swallow Gardens and, turning on his lamp, discovered Frances Coles lying on the ground, surrounded by a pool of blood. Despite her throat having been cut she was still alive – just – and as PC Thompson looked he saw the faint movement of one eyelid.

As Police Orders dictated an officer remain with a victim should they be alive, Thompson was unable to pursue the footsteps and the probable killer of Frances Coles – and possibly Jack the Ripper. She soon died from her wounds.

Very soon the archway of Swallow Gardens was filled with police officers and medical men, and closed off to the public. A thorough examination of the area was made, and in a space between a waterpipe and some brickwork two shillings wrapped in a piece of newspaper were discovered; whether these had been put there by the victim was impossible to prove.

While it is unlikely that Frances Coles was a victim

*The entrance to Swallow Gardens from Chamber Street
Inset: Frances Coles and the man arrested for her murder,
James Sadler*

of Jack the Ripper, hers is the last case of the eleven included in the police file of Whitechapel murders.

According to his family, PC Thompson was haunted

by his failure to catch the Ripper. He was murdered in 1900, stabbed to death after attempting to break up a disturbance at a Whitechapel coffee stall.

☞ *Resume walking along Chamber Street, pass under the railway bridge, and at the end turn right and veer left across the first set of traffic lights. Walk over the island and across the next set of traffic lights, so that you're walking along Goodman's Yard on the opposite side of the road to the Travelodge hotel. At the end of Goodman's Yard follow the path right into Minories. Walk all the way up Minories on the right-hand side, until near the very end, then slip right into Golden Fleece Court on your right.*

---

27. "MURDER!"

In the early hours of 18th September, a week after the murder of Annie Chapman and with the East End in a state of extreme nervousness, PC Johnson of the City of London Police was walking his beat along Minories when he heard a loud cry of "Murder!" It came from the notorious Three Kings' Court, now long-gone but just a few feet to the south of where you are now standing in this similarly-secluded court.

Hurrying through the alleyway that led into the

court from Minories, Johnson found a man and a woman standing together. When asked what he was doing, the man gave the brusque reply 'Nothing.' The woman was evidently terrified, and begged 'Oh policeman, do take me out of this!"

Johnson escorted the couple out of the court and told the man to be on his way. As he disappeared into the night, the woman turned to Johnson and exclaimed "Dear me. He frightened me very much when he pulled that big knife out." Johnson's jaw no doubt fell open. "Why didn't you tell me that at the time?" he asked. "I was too much frightened."

The officer conducted a quick search of the area but could find no trace of the man. As it transpired, he had headed over to a coffee-stall on Whitechapel High Street, where he got into a heated exchange with a youth named Alexander Finlay. Having pulled out a long-bladed knife, the man chased Finlay around the coffee stall and attempted to stab him, whereupon a constable arrived and took the man into police custody.

His name was Charles Ludwig, a hairdresser employed on the Minories, and immediately the police considered him a good contender for being the Whitechapel murder. He was remanded in custody while his background was looked into, but his innocence of the murders was proved conclusively when, in the early hours of 30th September and with Ludwig safely in custody, the killer struck again and thereby absolved him of any involvement.

Exit Golden Fleece Court back onto Minories, then turn right and pause at the junction with Aldgate High Street to look over at

28. ST BOTOLPH'S CHURCH

Built in 1740 to the design of George Dance the Elder, this church was something of a local landmark at the time of the Ripper murders. However, the oft-repeated tradition that the island on which the church is located was known as 'Prostitute island' in the 19th century is, as far as can be ascertained, nothing more than an urban legend, albeit one that is widely circulated as an established fact!

At around 8.30pm on 29th September 1888, City of London Constable Louis Robinson noticed a crowd gathering on the stretch of Aldgate High Street to the right of the church. Pushing through them, he found a woman, whom he later identified as Catherine Eddowes, lying on the pavement, drunk. He asked the crowd if any of them knew who she was, but got

no answer. Lifting her to her feet, he carried her over to the shutters of one of the shops where he propped her against them. She promptly slithered down to the ground. With the assistance of a fellow policeman, PC Robinson managed to manhandle her to Bishopsgate Police Station where she was asked her name, to which she replied "Nothing." She was locked up in one of the cells to sleep off her excesses.

George Hutt, the City gaoler, came on duty at 10.00pm. He checked on her several times over the next few hours, and each time she was sleeping soundly. However, by 12.15am, on the morning of the 30th, she had awoken and Hutt heard her singing softly to herself. Fifteen minutes later she called to him and asked when she would be allowed to leave. "When you can take care of yourself," Hutt called back. "I can do that now," came her reply.

At 12.55am he brought her from the cell and told her she could go. When asked her name and address for the release papers, she replied 'Mary Ann Kelly of 6 Fashion Street.' Discharging her from custody, Hutt pushed open the swing door to the passage and said "This way, Missus."

As she walked along the passage to the outer door, she asked him what time it was. "Too late for you to get anymore drink," observed Hutt. "I shall get a damned fine hiding when I get home," she sighed as she opened the door. Hutt was not in the least bit sympathetic. "And serve you right," he replied. "You have no right to get drunk."

As Kate left the station, Hutt asked her to shut the door behind her. "All right," she chirped. "Good Night Old Cock." She was murdered within the hour.

Go left along Aldgate High Street, crossing the Minories, and cross the road at the traffic lights then head left towards the red-bricked school, and pass through Aldgate Square with the school to your left. Pause on the corner of

29. ST JAMES'S PASSAGE

In 1888 known as Church Passage, a much narrower alleyway before the regeneration of recent years, this was one of three entrances into Mitre Square, a large but lonely courtyard surrounded by tall warehouses and therefore quiet at night, where Catherine Eddowes was murdered just 45 minutes after Elizabeth Stride in what became known as the 'Double Event'.

At 1.30am in the early hours of 30th September 1888, three friends were preparing to leave the Imperial Club, a members' club for local businessmen at 16&17 Duke Street. It was on the opposite side of the street to the Great Synagogue, which bordered Church Passage on its right-hand side.

Departing the Club three or four minutes later, as the three men walked south towards Aldgate one of them – commercial traveller Joseph Lawende – was a short distance ahead of his colleagues, butcher Joseph Hyam Levy and furniture dealer Harry Harris. After walking parallel to the Great Synagogue for some 15 feet they approached the turn into Church Passage at 1.35am, and saw a man and a woman standing under

The Great Synagogue on Duke Street, with the entrance to Church Passage indicated by a white star

the gas lamp above its entrance. She was standing with her back to the trio, so they were unable to see her face, but Lawende would later identify her by her clothes. It was, almost certainly, Catherine Eddowes. Hyam Levy also saw the couple, and commented to Harris: "Here, I'm off. I don't like the look of those people over there. I don't like going home by myself at this hour of the morning. I don't like passing this class of persons." The three men walked on towards their respective homes, none of them looking back at the couple.

Five minutes later City policeman PC James Harvey passed by on his beat. The couple had by this time left their post at the entrance to Church Passage, and Harvey saw nobody about; he went down the passage, checking the doors of premises on either side as he did so. At the end of Church Passage he turned and walked back up the 5ft-wide thoroughfare and then back into Duke Street, noticing nothing suspicious.

Walk down St James's Passage and pause on the left by the board on the wall, on which you will see a section that remembers the murder of Catherine Eddowes – making her unique amongst the victims as the only one to have any official recognition at the site of her murder. Keep ahead to reach the gated entrance to Sir John Cass School, and pause with your back to the gates.

30. THE DISCOVERY OF CATHERINE EDDOWES'S BODY

At 1.44am – just a few minutes after PC Harvey had completed his examination of Church Passage – PC Alfred Watkins turned out of Leadenhall Street, strolled along Mitre Street, and veered right into Mitre Square. Almost immediately he discovered the

Mitre Square. Catherine Eddowes's body was found where indicated by the white star

body of Catherine Eddowes, the gloom lifted by the soft glow of his Bullseye lamp.

Racing across the square, Watkins burst into Kearley

and Tonge's warehouse, where he knew that George Morris, a retired policeman, was working as a night watchman. "For God's sake mate," cried Watkins, "come to my assistance... here is another woman cut to pieces." Pausing momentarily to get his lamp, the night watchman followed Watkins to the square's south west corner, took one look at the body, and raced off along Mitre Street towards Aldgate, blowing furiously on his whistle to raise the alarm.

Within moments police were converging on Mitre Square, where an horrific sight awaited them. Catherine was lying on her back in a pool of blood, her head turned toward her left shoulder, and her clothes thrown up over her waist. Her abdomen had been cut open, and most of the intestines had been drawn out and placed over her right shoulder, whilst a severed two foot-long section of them had been placed between the body and the left arm. Her throat had been cut. 'V'-shaped cuts had been carved into her cheeks and eyelids; her nose had been all but cut off, and the lobe of the right ear had been cut through.

Missing from the body were the uterus and the left kidney. The killer had also removed a piece of the white apron that she was wearing, apparently taking it away with him, as it was missing from the scene.

Cross diagonally left across the square and exit it via the covered passage. Turn right along Creechurch Lane. Cross over at the traffic lights, keeping ahead through the continuation of Creechurch Lane, go left and cross Houndsditch via the traffic lights crossing, veering right on the other side, and then turn left along Stoney Lane. Turn left into White Kennett Street, and then turn right along Harrow Place. At the end of Harrow Place turn right into Middlesex Street. Walk past the stepped entrance to the concrete flats and pause by the two telephone boxes. Behind you on, the right, is the site of

....

31. 36 MIDDLESEX STREET

The home of Ripper suspect Jacob Levy. Aged 32 at the time of the murders, Levy was a butcher who, in his youth, had discovered the body of his brother Abraham, who had hanged himself. He took over his aunt's butchery business here at 36 Middlesex Street in 1883, and in 1886 was found guilty of stealing meat from a neighbouring business, being sentenced to 12 months' imprisonment but soon deemed insane and transferred to a lunatic asylum.

He returned to Middlesex Street in 1887 and resumed his butchering trade, but, following the death of his mother in May 1888, his mental health

Middlesex Street looking south, the junction with what is now Harrow Place plastered with advertisements. No. 36, home to Jacob Levy, is obscured by the streetlamp but marked with a white star.

deteriorated again and he was eventually admitted to another asylum, where he died in 1891.

Middlesex Street is also of note as it marks the boundary between the Metropolitan and City of London Police forces, the territories keenly observed. The City force resisted efforts for it to be absorbed into the surrounding Metropolitan Police district, which governs the whole of London expect this one square mile. When the boundaries between the two were formally agreed, one commentator complained that criminals "would assemble in the City of London as an asylum. When they throw a dog into the water, the fleas all get onto the head to avoid drowning, and in the same way all the thieves would get into the City to avoid hanging."

Despite this uneasy relationship, the two forces worked closely together during the Ripper investigation once the City had been brought in as a result of the murder of Catherine Eddowes on their territory.

Cross over Middlesex Street via the Zebra crossing and turn right, then turn left at the Bell pub into New Goulston Street. At its end turn left into Goulston Street and cross to the large brown-brick block, then pause at the doorway of the Happy Days fish and chip shop.

32. THE CLUE AT GOULSTON STREET

It was in this doorway that PC Alfred Long found the missing piece of Catherine's apron as he was on his beat along Goulston Street at 2.55am on 30th September 1888. Walking past the doorway that led to the staircases of 108 to 119 Wentworth Model Dwellings, he noticed the portion of apron lying on the floor inside the doorway. On closer inspection he discovered that it was covered with blood and faeces, and there were other marks that were suggestive that the blade of a knife having been wiped on it.

PC Long had, in fact, walked past the same doorway at 2.20am, and was emphatic that he would, most certainly, have noticed had the piece of apron been there then; he was, therefore, sure that it hadn't been there at that time.

The apron is the only real clue that Jack the Ripper left behind, and it tells us much about the killer's intentions and appearance as he fled the scene of his latest atrocity, but, at the same time, it also raises other questions that, in some ways, muddy the waters even further!

It is a clue insomuch as it reveals to us the direction that the Ripper took as he fled from Mitre Square in the wake of his murder of Catherine Eddowes. There can be no doubt that he was going to ground as he headed away from the murder scene, so the location of the bloodied fragment suggests the route his took as he headed to his home, or a bolt-hole.

The apron also answers the question of the killer's appearance as he fled from the scenes of his atrocities. There is a common belief that he must have been drenched in blood, having carried out such brutal

The entrance to 108-119 Wentworth Model Dwellings. The apron piece was found on the floor to the right, with the graffito on the black wall above

and gruesome murders. But this was, probably, not the case. Indeed, the apron tells us how much visible and incriminating blood he would have had upon his person, for, as he made his way through the streets, he would undoubtedly have had blood on his hands and on the blade of his knife, and would have been anxious to wipe this away as soon as possible. Had he stopped in the streets and wiped away the evidence, he may have been noticed. He required some cover to perform this task, and a recessed and dark doorway, such as this one in Goulston Street, would have provided sufficient privacy for him to wipe his hands and the blade of his knife without attracting any attention to his nefarious task. Once he was certain that he was clean enough, he would have dropped the apron and continued home.

Long's first thought, on discovering the portion of apron, was that someone may have been attacked and could at that very moment be lying injured or dead on a staircase or landing inside the dwellings. He stood up, intending to search the block. As he did so, he noticed a scrawled chalk message on the wall directly above the apron. It read, "The Juwes are the men that will not be blamed for nothing." Summoning a fellow officer to guard the scene, PC Long hurried to Commercial Street Police Station to report his find and to hand in the piece of apron.

Soon, officers of the Metropolitan Police were gathering around the doorway and gazing at the 'Juwes' graffiti with feelings of great trepidation. Mindful of the strong feelings of anti-Semitism that had surfaced in the area in the wake of the 'Leather Apron' scare, and realizing that Wentworth Model Dwellings not only stood in a largely Jewish locality, but was also inhabited almost exclusively by Jews, the Metropolitan Police began to fear that, if the message was left intact, it could lead to a resurgence of racial unrest in the district, and the consequences could be dire. They were therefore anxious to erase the message, and to do so sooner rather than later.

But both the portion of apron and the graffiti pertained to a murder investigation being carried out by the City Police, detectives of which had soon crossed the boundary and were also gathering around the doorway. They were not so keen to erase what they saw as an important clue in their investigation, and the two forces clashed over what should be done about the graffito. The City Police were adamant that it should be photographed. The Metropolitan Police pointed out that would mean waiting until it was light, by which time Gentile purchasers would be arriving in their thousands to purchase from the Jewish stallholders at the Petticoat Lane and Goulston Street Sunday markets.

Since there was no way of keeping it hidden from these crowds, the Metropolitan Police were convinced the result might be a full-scale riot against the Jews. A compromise was suggested by the City whereby only the top line – "The Juwes are" – would be erased. But, as Superintendent Arnold of the Metropolitan Police later pointed out in a report, "Had only a portion of the writing been removed the context would have remained."

The bickering was still going on when Metropolitan Police Commissioner Sir Charles Warren arrived at the scene between 5.00 and 5.30am. Since the doorway stood on Metropolitan Police territory his word was final, and he immediately concurred with his officers that leaving the graffito any longer would lead to far greater crimes against innocent Jews. He ordered that the message be erased without delay, and before any photograph of it could be taken. It would prove once of the most controversial orders he gave in the entire investigation.

Resume walking along Goulston Street to the corner and turn right along Wentworth Street, then take the next right into Old Castle Street and keep ahead until you come to the surviving façade of the former Wash Houses on the right. This is the location of

33. THE MURDER OF ALICE MCKENZIE

In 1889 Old Castle Street was named Castle Alley, and was much narrower than today. At 12.20am on 17th July that year, PC Walter Andrews was walking his beat and passed through Castle Alley, seeing nothing to attract his attention. At 12.30am PC Allen entered the street and stopped for five minutes under a lamp outside some offices, approximately where the entrance to the more modern block is now, to enjoy some supper. He too noticed nothing suspicious, and on finishing his food went back to his duty.

At 12.48am PC Andrews returned to Castle Alley on another circuit, when Sergeant Badham approached on his check of the patrols. On receiving the "Alright" he left Andrews, but had gone no further than 150 yards when he heard the shrill blast of the constable's whistle. He rushed back to Castle Alley and found PC Andrews standing over the body of a woman, a pool of blood around her head and her skirts pushed up to expose her abdomen. She was lying under the very lamp at which PC Allen had enjoyed his supper.

Allen was alerted by Sgt. Badham and went to fetch Dr. Bagster Phillips, while PC Andrews remained with the body. He touched it, and felt that it was quite warm. Dr. Phillips arrived at 1.10am and conducted

DISCOVERY OF THE BODY OF ALICE MACKENZIE IN CASTLE-ALLEY, WHITECHAPEL.

an examination; the victim was lying on her back, with her face turned to the right. Her eyelids were open, her pupils dilated. There were two deep wounds in the left side of the neck, from which a large amount of blood had flowed into the gutter.

The body was removed to the mortuary, and at two o'clock that same afternoon Dr. Phillips conducted a post mortem, the victim by now having been identified as Alice McKenzie. Death had been caused by the wounds to the throat, and seven or eight superficial wounds to the stomach and pubic area indicated an attempt at mutilation.

Had the close proximity of two beat constables frightened the killer into abandoning his plans of evisceration? There were just fifteen minutes between PC Allen finishing his supper and departing, and PC Andrews returning to that spot at 12.50am. Did Andrews disturb the killer? If so, was the culprit saved from capture by the intervention of Sergeant Badham spending a minute or two with Andrews? Dr Thomas Bond, who six months earlier had written a report naming which victims he believed to have been killed by Jack the Ripper, was of the opinion that Alice McKenzie was slain by the same hand.

Continue along Old Castle Street, turn left into Pomell Way, then left in Commercial Street. Keep ahead to the traffic lights and pause to look across at the Culpeper public house. In 1888 this was

34. THE PRINCESS ALICE

First constructed in 1846 and then rebuilt in 1883 as a result of the widening of Wentworth Street, the pub was named after Queen Victoria's second daughter, who had been born three years earlier.

It was at the Princess Alice that victim Frances Coles met James Sadler on the evening of 11th February

1889, he having just been discharged from his duties as ship's fireman on the SS *Fez*.

The pair went on a tour of the pubs of Spitalfields and Whitechapel over the next couple of days, and late in the evening of 12th February had a drunken argument after Frances refused to go to Sadler's aid when he was attacked and robbed, and they went their separate ways.

At 1.30am, after an hour of aimlessly wandering the streets, Frances was back by the Princess Alice, where she bumped into a friend named Ellen Callana, who, like Frances, was known to be a prostitute. As they walked together in the direction of the Minories, "a very short man with a dark moustache, shiny boots and blue trousers" approached Callana and solicited her; she refused his offer, at which the man punched her in the face and tore her jacket. He then walked over to Frances, who, unbelievably ignoring the assault on her friend, walked away with the stranger in the direction of Swallow Gardens and her doom.

The vicinity around the Princess Alice was also allegedly frequented by the mysterious 'Leather Apron'. On asking two local women for his whereabouts, a reporter from the tabloid newspaper the *Star* was directed by one to this spot on "Commercial Street, opposite the Princess Alice tavern, as the most

Edgar's Guide To...

The Princess Alice in the 1950s

likely place to find him... she added that it would be necessary to look into all the shadows, as if he was there he would surely be out of sight."

The Princess Alice was renamed the City Darts in 1986 and its upstairs function room was the long-time venue for Whitechapel Society meetings, before being refurbished and reverting to its original name in 2005. The interior was gutted and completely refitted in 2014 and reopened as the Culpeper.

Cross over the traffic lights towards the Culpeper, on the other side turning right to walk along Commercial Street, turning left into the courtyard of

35. TOYNBEE HALL

Toynbee Hall was founded in 1884 by the Reverend Samuel Barnett and his wife Henrietta to provide a place where wealthy young men, destined to become future leaders, would live and work amongst the poor of the area, thus confronting them with first-hand experience of poverty and hardship in the hope that they might come up with practical solutions for stamping it out.

In the wake of the murder of Martha Tabram,

unimpressed by the police endeavours to catch the perpetrator, seventy local residents held a meeting at Toynbee Hall at which they formed the St Jude's Vigilance Committee that would work out of Toynbee Hall. Twelve men were appointed to act as 'watchers', tasked with observing certain streets between the hours of 11.00pm and 1.00am, providing support to the local police whenever necessary and to report to the Committee on disorderly houses and those who caused disturbances in the neighbourhood.

This was the precursor of several such vigilance committees, the most famous of which was the Mile End Vigilance Committee, the president of which was local builder George Lusk, the recipient of the notorious 'From Hell' letter.

Backtrack to the Culpeper and go over Wentworth Street, walking along Commercial Street, and cross over Thrawl Street and Lolesworth Close, continuing until you come to the junction with Fashion Street.

36. THE FORMER QUEEN'S HEAD

The building formerly known as the Queen's Head pub has re-appeared under its original name in recent years.

As far as can be established, there was a pub on this site since the early 19th century, although the evidence suggests that the current building was built in the 1850s.

It served its last pint in 1927 and has, since then, gone through a series of incarnations, a bank and a confectioner's shop to name but two of them. In 2014 the building was taken over by the architectural practice of Chris Dyson, who restored it and chose to restore its façade – though not its interior – as a public house, complete with the Queen's Head signage that you can see on the upper storeys.

It was in the Queen's Head that Elizabeth Stride began her last night alive, for she was seen in the pub at 6.30pm on the evening of 29th September 1888.

It was also under the street light outside this pub that George Hutchinson stood in the early hours of 9th November 1888 to watch Mary Kelly, whose murder we will come to shortly, walk past him with a man on their way to Dorset Street. As they passed him, the man, so Hutchinson later recalled, "hung his head down with his hat over his eyes. I stooped down and looked him in the face. He looked at me stern."

It was also at the Queen's Head that, on the evening of Annie Chapman's murder, a woman, whose name was only given as Lyons, whom the newspapers

A contemporary sketch of George Hutchinson watching Mary Kelly and her companion

described as being "of the class commonly known as unfortunates", had an alarming encounter with a sinister man.

According to a newspaper account:

"She stated that at three o'clock on the Saturday afternoon she met a strange man in Flower and Dean Street, one of the worst streets in the East End of London. He asked her to go to Queen's Head public-house at half-past six and drink with him. Having obtained from the young woman a promise that she would do so he disappeared, but was at the house at the appointed time.

While they were conversing, Lyons noticed a large

knife in his right-hand trousers pocket, and called another woman's attention to the fact.

A moment later, Lyons was startled by a remark which the stranger addressed to her. "You are about the same style of woman as the one that's murdered," he said. "What do you know about her?" asked the woman, to which the man replied, "You are beginning to smell a rat. Foxes hunt geese, but they don't always find 'em." Having uttered these words, the man hurriedly left.

Lyons followed until near Spitalfields Church, and turning round at this spot, and noticing that the woman was behind him, the stranger ran swiftly into Church Street, and was lost from sight.

One noteworthy fact in this story is that the description of the man's appearance is in all material points identical with the published description of the unknown and, up to the present, undiscovered Leather Apron."

Let's now follow in her footsteps as she left the Queen's Head in pursuit of the mysterious character.

> *Continue walking along Commercial Street and pause at the gates of*

37. CHRIST CHURCH SPITALFIELDS

Considered his masterpiece, Christ Church Spitalfields was built between 1714 and 1729 to a design by Nicholas Hawksmoor. It is one of East London's most famous landmarks, and a reminder of the former splendour of Spitalfields before the area's decline in the mid-1800s.

After two centuries of worship the fabric of the church began to deteriorate, and by the 1950s the roof was considered too dangerous to allow services to be held. Demolition was averted thanks to the efforts of the Hawksmoor Committee, who raised awareness of the church's predicament, and the roof was rebuilt in 1966. The Friends of Christ Church Spitalfields group was formed in 1976 to help restore the church to its former glories, and ten years later services were once again held at Christ Church Spitalfields.

To the left of the church runs Fournier Street, built in the mid-1720s as Church Street. On the corner of Fournier Street and Commercial Street is the famous Ten Bells public house, of which more later.

No. 3 Fournier Street, which bears the signage W.&A. Jones, is an important location in the story of victim Catherine Eddowes and her partner, John Kelly. The couple had returned to Whitechapel the previous day after hop-picking in Kent, as many East Enders did in

Jones's pawnbrokers, with the canopy, in the shadow of Christ Church. The Ten Bells is out of shot to the left.

the summer months to earn some money.

Although they had lived together for seven years at Cooney's Lodging House on Flower and Dean Street, as they were penniless that night they both slept at the Casual Ward on Shoe Lane.

The following day John managed to earn sixpence through labouring, so while he spent 4d on a single bed at Cooney's, with Catherine taking the remaining 2d and heading for the Casual Ward at Mile End.

They met the following morning at 8 o'clock, and Kate pawned John's boots with Mr. Jones at this shop on Church Street in the shadow of Christ Church, fetching 2s 6d, some of which they spent on supplies of tea and sugar to be kept on her person by Kate, and the rest on breakfast, which they ate at Cooney's between 10.00 and 11.00 o'clock.

After their welcome meal the couple once again found themselves without any money, so Kate suggested that she go to Bermondsey to see whether she could find her daughter Annie and borrow some.

They parted on Houndsditch at 2 o'clock, Kate promising John that she would be back within a couple of hours. He never saw her alive again.

....

Cross Fournier Street and continue along Commercial Street, past the Ten Bells, and keep ahead over Hanbury Street and Jerome Street. As you walk along Commercial Street, on its opposite side is the first Peabody Dwelling, housing built specifically for the working poor, which opened in 1864. Keep ahead along Commercial Street, passing the Commercial Tavern, and just after it pause to look over Commercial Street at

38. THE FORMER COMMERCIAL STREET POLICE STATION

Built in 1876, this odd-shaped police station was apparently known by officers who served here as 'Comical Street'. Along with Leman Street Police Station in Whitechapel, it was here that the local investigation into the Ripper murders was conducted. This was the station to which John Davis ran after discovering the body of Annie Chapman, PC Alfred Long took the only clue – the bloodied portion of Catherine Eddowes apron – and John McCarthy and Thomas Bower went to report the murder of Mary Kelly.

Inspector Frederick Abberline was the most famous of the detectives based here at Commercial Street Police Station during the murders.

An extra storey was added in 1907 to provide additional accommodation. When the old Leman Street Police Station was demolished in 1967, staff there moved to Commercial Street station while the new facilities were being built. On their completion in March 1970 all business was transferred back to

Leman Street, with Commercial Street Police Station closing to become private accommodation. Today it is flats called Burhan Uddin House.

Backtrack past the Commercial Tavern, and at the Costa Coffee shop cross at the traffic lights to walk down Commercial Street past the Peabody Dwelling. Cross Folgate Street and then Lamb Street, passing Spitalfields Market, which opened in 1887, the year before the Ripper murders, to celebrate Queen Victoria's Golden Jubilee. Once past the market turn right into Brushfield Street and cross to its left side, passing the Fruit and Wool Exchange building on your left. Cross over Crispin Street, making sure to notice the colourful frontage of Donovan Bros. Paper Bag Makers. A little further along Brushfield Street, at the Verde & Co. property, turn left into Gun Street, where in 1888 was situated

39. MR TENPENNY'S LODGING HOUSE

On the evening of 16th July 1889 a labourer named John McCormack arrived back at his lodgings at 52 Gun Street, more commonly known as 'Tenpenny's' after the owner, Mr. Thomas Tempany, from his job at a Jewish tailors on Hanbury Street. It was four o'clock,

Gun Street in 1890

and after giving some money to his common-law wife Alice McKenzie he retired to bed for a few hours.

When McCormack woke around 11.00 o'clock Alice

had gone out. Deputy Betsy Ryder had seen her walk through the kitchen and out the front door onto Gun Street at around 8.30pm.

The next definite sighting of Alice McKenzie came at 11.40pm. Margaret Franklin, who had known her for many years, was sitting on the step of a barber's shop at Flower and Dean Street when Alice walked past, heading in the direction of Whitechapel. She paused briefly to talk then continued on her way. The body of Alice McKenzie was discovered just over an hour later in Castle Alley.

Mr. Tempany shared the cost of her funeral with the landlord of The Tower public house, which stood nearby on Artillery Lane.

Large enough to host 198 lodgers, 'Tenpenny's' was situated on the right-hand side towards the end of Gun Street, where the beige-brick building numbered 51-53 now stands. It was demolished in the early 1970s.

....

Continue to the end of Gun Street and go left along Artillery Lane, cross to its right side, and go right through the bollards to squeeze through the wonderfully atmospheric Artillery Passage, pausing by the red-painted doorway opposite the King's Stores pub when you emerge onto Sandys Row. The opposite corner to the King's Stores, in front of the narrow building numbered '17', was where

40. MRS PAUMIER HAD A FRIGHTENING ENCOUNTER

On the morning following the murder of Mary Kelly, a young woman named Annie Paumier was selling roasted chestnuts when a man she described as having a 'gentlemanly' appearance approached and asked whether she had heard about the murder. When Mrs. Paumier replied that she had, the man grinned and said "I know more about it than you." He then stared into her face before heading off up Sandy's Row, to your right, pausing at the end to look back to see if she was watching him.

Mrs. Paumier said he was carrying the by-now expected black shiny bag, about a foot wide and a foot-and-a-half in length.

> *Turn left before the King Stores to walk along Sandy's Row, and take the first left into the pedestrianised Frying Pan Alley, emerging at its end onto Bell Lane. Cross to the opposite side and turn left, then pause at the corner with White's Row to look across at the yellow-bricked*

41. PROVIDENCE ROW NIGHT SHELTER

Built in 1868, and run by the Sisters of Mercy who provided lodging "to the destitute of all parts, without distinction of creed, colour, and country." Among those reputed to have taken shelter here was Ripper suspect Francis Thompson.

There was, according to a 1973 episode of the BBC series *Timewatch* entitled 'Shadow of the Ripper', a tradition amongst the nuns at the Refuge that Mary Kelly had stayed here briefly before being found a position as a domestic servant, from which she absconded and took to earning a living on the streets. The programme's makers interviewed an elderly nun who, in 1915, had been a novice at Providence Row, She recalled that the refuge "was opposite the pub where Kelly and Chapman rubbed shoulders daily" (the pub in question being the Horn of Plenty). She

PROVIDENCE ROW NIGHT REF
MALE AND FEMALE APPLIC.

also quoted an old sister, who was a resident of the convent in 1888, who had told her: "If it had not been for the Kelly woman, none of the murders would have happened."

Turn right into White's Row, cross to its left and pause at the bottom of the steps on the left-hand side which lead into the modern office block. Opposite you, with four blue-painted metal balcony railings, is the site of

42. SPITALFIELDS CHAMBERS

A respectable name for what was by 1888 a run-down lodging house at 8 White's Row, Spitalfields Chambers was where victim Frances Coles spent the night of 11th February 1891 with James Sadler, the couple meeting there again the following evening. As Sadler had been earlier robbed and beaten in Thrawl Street, both were penniless and therefore forced to leave, going their separate ways. Frances wandered off to her death two hours later in Swallow Gardens.

Spitalfields Chambers was also home to Annie Millwood, the victim of a possible early attack by the Ripper. She was admitted into the Whitechapel Workhouse Infirmary on 25th February 1888 with "numerous stabs in the legs and lower part of the body," having been attacked by a man she did not know. Although she initially recovered, Annie died of natural causes five weeks later.

Spitalfields Chambers was demolished in the late 20th century and replaced by this present building in the 1990s.

Go up the steps to enter the courtyard of the office block and pause at the centre.

43. DORSET STREET AND THE MURDER OF MARY KELLY

You are now standing, more or less, on the site of Dorset Street, a thoroughfare that in 1888 was lined with common lodging houses, and which had such a reputation for poverty, vice and criminality that it was widely known as "the worst street in London."

Running off Dorset Street were several courts, one of which was Miller's Court, reached via an arched

Dorset Street

The entrance to Miller's Court from Dorset Street, just behind the chair, with John McCarthy's chandlers shop to it left

passage between numbers 26 and 27, both of which were owned by shopkeeper and slum landlord, John McCarthy, who also rented out several rooms in the court itself behind the buildings.

The passage was about 20 feet long, and on the right, just before it opened out into the court, was the door to number 13, a tiny room that for eight months prior to November 1888 had been rented by 25-year-old Mary Kelly.

Until two weeks before her murder, she had been living there with an unemployed Billingsgate fish porter named Joseph Barnett. His lack of earnings meant that the rent on the room was in arrears, and Mary had resorted to prostitution. This led to arguments between them, and during one particularly heated exchange – apparently when Mary was tipsy – a pane of glass in the window by the door had been broken. The window was stuffed with newspaper and rags, and was covered by an old coat. Then, in late October, Mary had invited a homeless prostitute named Julia to stay with them. This proved too much for Barnett, who decided enough was enough and moved out.

Joe Barnett had remained on friendly terms with Mary, and he had last seen her alive when he called on her between 7.00 and 8.00pm on Thursday, 8th

November.

One of the last sightings of her was at 2.00am on the morning of 9th November, when George Hutchinson met her on Commercial Street. She asked him for sixpence. He declined on account of the fact he was 'spent up'. Mary continued along Commercial Street and began talking with a man near the junction with Thrawl Street. The two then backtracked along Commercial Street, and Hutchinson followed them along Dorset Street and watched as Mary Kelly led the man into Miller's Court. Hutchinson waited on the other side of Dorset Street for 45 minutes, but neither the man nor Mary Kelly emerged, so he left.

At around 4.00am on the morning of 9th November two neighbours in Miller's Court claimed that they had heard a faint cry of "Oh, Murder!" But cries of "Murder" were quite a regular occurrence in the neighbourhood, and often meant a drunken brawl or domestic violence was occurring, so it was customary for those on the receiving end of such violence to scream out the word. The local residents, not wishing to get involved, would ignore such cries, which is exactly what the two neighbours did on hearing the cry that night in Miller's Court.

At 10.45am that morning Mary Kelly's landlord, John McCarthy, sent his assistant Thomas Bowyer –

The police photograph of 13 Miller's Court, home to Mary Kelly

who was also known as 'Indian Harry' – round to 13 Miller's Court to collect her overdue rent. Striding into the court Bowyer banged twice on her door but got no answer. No doubt believing that she was inside but unwilling or unable to pay her rent, Bowyer stepped around the corner and pulled aside a curtain that covered the broken window pane.

Moments later an ashen-faced Bowyer staggered back into McCarthy's shop. "Guv'nor," he spluttered, "I knocked at the door and could not make anyone answer. I looked through the window and saw a lot of blood." "You don't mean that, Harry…" was McCarthy's horrified response, and the two men hurried from the shop and into Miller's Court. Stooping down, McCarthy pushed aside the curtain and gazed into the gloomy room. A sight of unimaginable horror met his eyes. The wall behind the bed was spattered with blood. On the bedside table was a pile of bloody human flesh. And there, on the bed, lay the virtually skinned cadaver of Mary Kelly.

"The sight that we saw I cannot drive away from my mind," McCarthy later told a journalist. "It looked more like the work of a devil than of a man… I hope I may never see such a sight as this again."

That sight was the only one of Jack the Ripper's victims to be photographed *in situ*, and is believed to be the world's first murder scene photograph. Reproduced opposite, the image shows the full horror of the extensive mutilations carried out on the body of poor Mary Kelly.

Jack the Ripper's East End

And, although the Whitechapel murders would continue for several more years, it is generally accepted that Mary Kelly was the last victim of the killer that we know as Jack the Ripper.

Continue through the courtyard and exit to turn right along Brushfield Street. At the end go left along Commercial Street and cross it via the pedestrian crossing to end your tour at

44. THE TEN BELLS

If there is one pub that, more than any other, is synonymous with the Jack the Ripper case, this pub is it! Dating from the mid-18th century, the pub's landlord in 1888 was John Waldron, and several victims of Jack the Ripper were reputedly amongst his regular clientele. Tradition holds that it was Mary Kelly's local, and there are unsubstantiated claims that patrons of the pub sent flowers for her funeral. There were, again uncorroborated, rumours that Annie Chapman had been seen drinking in the pub by its pot-man at 5.00am, just one hour before her body was found in nearby Hanbury Street, and she was apparently summoned by a man who popped his head round the door and beckoned her out.

What is certain is that the pub was so associated with the case that, from 1976 to 1988, it actually changed its name from the Ten Bells to the Jack the Ripper, and began trading on its notorious past; T-shirts, fridge magnets and a special 'Ripper Tipple' drink were all to be had here.

In recent years the pub has opted to distance itself from its Ripper-related past. Stepping inside, you are confronted by an interior that is similar to its appearance in 1888. Be sure to admire the tiled wall depicting Spitalfields in days of yore, one of a pair, with the other in the Whitechapel Gallery.

But, most of all, be sure to linger here, absorb its ambience and raise a glass to the memory of the eleven women whose stories you have followed over the course of your tour, and whose lives are a testimony to their resilience in the face of adversity that was thrown at them by a society that seemed to care little for the plight of the poor. I must leave you in their capable hands, my exhausted and footsore sleuths, so I wish you a pleasant remainder of your day, or night; get home safely, and when you retire to your beds later, do have sweet and pleasant dreams!

Pip, pip!

Edgar

A busy Commercial Street showing the Britannia pub on the left, which marked the entrance to Dorset Street

The Ten Bells above, with the flugpole on its roof. Christ Church is out of shot to the right

THE ELEVEN WHITECHAPEL MURDER VICTIMS

As mentioned earlier in this volume, as Jack the Ripper was never caught we don't know for sure how many victims were slain by the same hand.

The official Metropolitan Police file now held at the National Archives is titled the Whitechapel Murders, and contains the details of eleven murders between April 1888 and February 1891.

There were other attacks in the area which were linked to the Ripper by the press, no doubt in an attempt to sell newspapers, such as that on Annie Farmer, who survived a minor cut to the throat (and indeed may have inflicted it herself), and murders committed away from the East End but initially reported as the Ripper changing districts as Whitechapel had become 'too hot' for him.

Here, we present biographical information on all eleven victims in the official file, in chronological order, beginning with...

EMMA SMITH

Died 4th April 1888

Little is known of Emma Elizabeth Smith's history before 1888. Newspaper reports of the attack on her on 3rd April give her age as 45, and Inspector Edmund Reid describes her in his report as being 5ft 2in tall, with a fair complexion and light brown hair. She had a scar on her right temple. She may be the Emma Smith born Emma Elizabeth Binmore on Christmas Day 1843 in Devon, who grew up in Portsea and married Frederick Wells there in April 1862. On 1st September 1868 Emma Wells married a John Smith at Portsea; the couple are recorded as living at 118 Central Street, Finsbury in north London in the 1881 census. Victim Emma Smith told her neighbours in the lodging house that she had formerly lived in Finsbury with her family.

Although the attack itself, in Osborn Street, was not witnessed, Emma returned to the lodging house at 18 George Street, where she had lived for 18 months, between 4.00 and 5.00am on the morning of 3rd April with terrible injuries. Such was her condition that the Deputy, Mary Russell, immediately took her to the London Hospital where she was examined by House Surgeon Dr. George Haslip, who noted that her head was bruised and her right ear torn, in addition to a

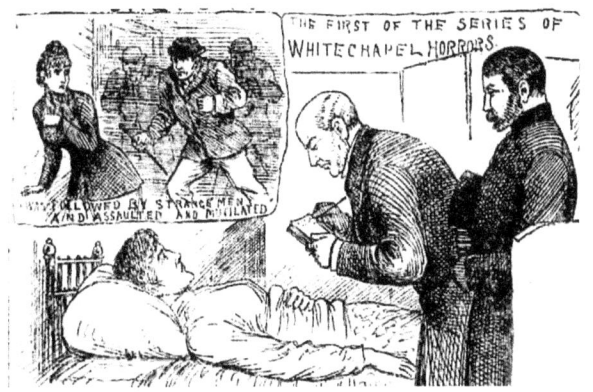

ruptured peritoneum and internal organs. Emma told Dr. Haslip that she had been passing St. Mary's Church on Whitechapel Road at 1.30am when she saw two or three men approaching her, so she crossed the road to avoid them. The men followed her up Osborn Street and robbed and beat her, before inflicting the horrific fatal injury near the cocoa factory on the corner of Wentworth Street. Emma survived for just over 24 hours, dying at 9.00am on 4th April 1888.

The police were not informed of the incident until two days later, when they were told an inquest was to be held the next day at the London Hospital, to be presided over by Coroner Wynne Edwin Baxter.

As Emma had not described her assailants, and no

witnessed came forward, it was an impossible task and her attackers were never caught.

MARTHA TABRAM

Died 7th August 1888

Born Martha White on 10th May 1849 in Southwark, south London, Martha married widower Henry Samuel Tabram on Christmas Day 1869. The couple had two sons, Frederick (1871-1920) and Charles (1872-1956), before going their separate ways in 1875 due to Martha's heavy drinking.

Henry initially gave her an allowance of 12s a week but reduced it to 2s 6d; this was stopped completely when he discovered that she had begun living with another man, a carpenter named Henry Turner. He and Martha lived together on and off until July 1888, when they separated for the final time. Early reports of her murder often used the name 'Martha Turner'.

In his report into her murder, Inspector Ellisdon described her as being 37-years-old, 5ft 3in tall, with a dark complexion and dark hair. At the time of her death she was wearing a green skirt, a brown petticoat and a long black jacket, with brown stockings and a black bonnet.

Martha's last known abode was Satchell's Lodging House, 19 George Street. On 6th August 1888 she

was seen in various public houses with her friend of four months, a fellow prostitute named Mary Ann Connelly (aka 'Pearly Poll'). The pair were drinking with two guardsmen they had met in the Two Brewers on Brick Lane at around 10.00pm.

According to Connelly, the foursome separated around 11.45pm, with Martha and the Private disappearing into George Yard and she herself going with the Corporal up the parallel Angel Alley, no doubt both with the intention of having sex.

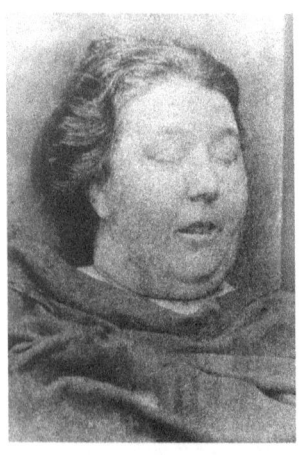

At 2.00am PC Thomas Barrett saw a Guardsman in Wentworth Street, at the north end of George Yard, who told him that he was "waiting for a chum who went off with a girl."

At about the same time a Mrs. Mahoney and her husband returned to their lodgings at George Yard Buildings and saw nothing suspicious, but when a cabman named Alfred Crow returned to his own rooms in George Yard Buildings at 3.30am he noticed 'something' on the landing. As it was not unusual for people to sleep where they could in the East End, including staircases, Crow thought nothing of it and continued to his bed.

The body of Martha Tabram was eventually discovered by John Reeves as he left his lodgings at 37 George Yard Buildings at 4.50am. Returning with PC Barrett, still on his beat, it was seen that Martha was lying on her back, legs open, with her arms by her side, fingers tightly clenched.

Dr. Timothy Killeen of nearby 68 Brick Lane arrived

at 5.30am and examined the body, estimating death to have occurred three hours earlier. She had been stabbed a total of 39 times in various places including her lungs, heart and stomach. All of the wounds had been inflicted while she had been alive.

In Dr. Killeen's opinion, all but one of the wounds could have been made with an 'ordinary penknife', with one wound to Martha's chest seemingly made by a sword, dagger or bayonet.

MARY ANN NICHOLS

Died 31st August 1888

Born Mary Ann Walker on 26th August 1845 to blacksmith Edward Walker and his wife Caroline in Dawes Court off Shoe Lane, Fleet Street, at the time of her death Mary Ann was reported as being 5ft 2in tall, with grey eyes, and brown hair turning grey. Several teeth were missing.

Known to all as 'Polly', she married William Nichols on 16th January 1864 at St Bride's Church in the City. They went on to have five children: Edward, Percy, Alice, Eliza and Henry.

After separating many times, the couple parted for the final time in 1881 and the following year William stopped the maintenance payments he had been making when he discovered Polly had started working

as a prostitute. As a result of the loss of regular income she endured several years of going in and out of the workhouse, and her dependency on alcohol increased.

In 1887 she found a position as a domestic servant at the Wandsworth home of Samuel and Sarah Cowdry, but two months later absconded having stolen clothing worth more than three pounds.

By early 1888 Polly had drifted to the East End, and was sharing a room with four other women at Wilmott's Lodging House at 18 Thrawl Street, Spitalfields. One of them, Emily Holland, was the last person to see Polly alive, when they met on the corner of Osborn Street and Whitechapel High Street.

Her body was found in Buck's Row, a ten minute

walk from Osborn Street. She was lying across the entrance to Brown's stableyard, next to which was a house called New Cottage. Despite her bedroom window overlooking the spot, Mrs Emma Green, who claimed to be a light sleeper, heard nothing all night until PC John Neil knocked on her door to ask whether she knew of the murder.

The manager of Essex Wharf opposite New Cottage, Walter Purkiss, said that neither he or his wife heard

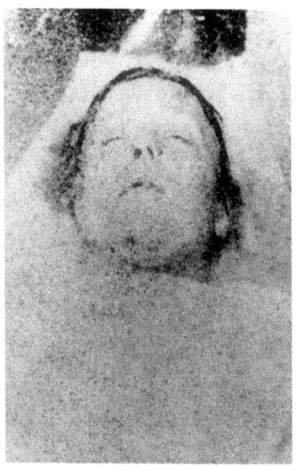

anything, despite both having been awake for some of the night.

ANNIE CHAPMAN

Died 8th September 1888

When the body of Annie Chapman was discovered in the Hanbury Street yard she was, of course, unknown, so the police made enquiries in the immediate area armed with the following physical description of the victim:

"Age 45, length 5 ft, complexion fair, hair (wavy) dark brown, eyes blue, two teeth deficient in lower jaw, large thick nose; dress black figured jacket, brown bodice, black skirt, lace boots, all old and dirty."

This resulted in an identification by Timothy Donovan, the Deputy of Crossingham's Lodging House at 35 Dorset Street. He had known the victim for around 16 months; she was a prostitute, and had lodged at Crossingham's for the previous four months. He knew her by the name 'Annie Siffey'.

It transpired that this unusual name was a result of Annie living for a while with a man who made iron sieves, and she was at that time widely known locally by the nickname 'Mrs Sivvey'. This was in 1886, and the couple had lived at 30 Dorset Street – another common lodging house – where they had made friends with Amelia Palmer and her husband Henry, an army pensioner who worked as a dock labourer. By early 1887 the sieve maker had left Annie, Mrs Palmer seeing him in the City and being told that he was now living in Notting Hill, west London.

Mrs Palmer was able to identify the Hanbury Street victim by her real name – Annie Chapman.

She had been born Annie Eliza Smith in September 1841 out of wedlock to 19-year-old George Smith and 22-year-old Ruth Chapman, who subsequently married at Paddington, north-west London five months later, on 22nd February 1842.

Following the marriage George and Ruth would go on to have six further children. George's service with

the 2nd Life Guards saw the family constantly relocate as he was stationed at various barracks between Knightsbridge and Windsor, west of London.

By the time of the 1861 census 19-year-old Annie had found employment, and was working as a housemaid to architect William Lewer at Duke Street in Westminster. But the suicide of her father in June 1863 saw her mother and younger siblings forced to move to 29 Montpelier Place in lower-middle class

Knightsbridge, an area well-populated with those in domestic service. To supplement the family's income Ruth let out rooms, and one such lodger was a gentleman's coachman named John Chapman.

On 1st May 1869 the 25-year-old John Chapman married Annie Smith, by then aged 27, at All Saints Church, Knightsbridge. The couple enjoyed a fairly comfortable lifestyle, with the accommodation provided with John's work seeing the family living in comfort in Bayswater, north west London, and then South Bruton Mews off Berkeley Square in Mayfair, and over the course of the next dozen years they welcomed several children into the family. By 1881 the family had moved to Windsor, where John took a job as a domestic coachman.

It would appear that Annie Chapman had always enjoyed a drink, but the death from meningitis of first born Emily Ruth in 1882 was the catalyst for her descent into heavy drinking. In December that year her sisters Miriam and Emily persuaded Annie to admit herself to the Spelthorne Sanatorium at Feltham to seek treatment, and she would spend a year there as a patient before returning home sober on 20th December 1883.

It would not take long for her to return to her old ways. Faced with dismissal from his job if he did not evict his wife from his lodgings, John Chapman realised he needed a regular income to care for the two young children who remained at home and took the latter decision.

The couple separated in 1884, Annie probably moving back to Knightsbridge to be with her mother and sisters, supported by a maintenance payment of 10s a week from her husband.

Over the course of the next two years Annie gradually made her way towards the East End, where she met the sieve maker, and soon found herself living in the common lodging houses of Spitalfields, predominantly those on Dorset Street.

Following John Chapman's sudden death on Christmas Day 1886 and the resulting cessation of her maintenance, Annie had sold flowers and undertaken crochet work to support herself, and on occasion resorting to casual prostitution to make ends meet.

By September 1888 she had been staying at 35 Dorset Street, Crossingham's Lodging House, for around four months. She had taken up with a bricklayer's labourer named Ted Stanley, who lived in lodgings of his own at 1 Osborn Street but would often visit Annie on a Saturday night, paying for a double bed for the two of them.

This was the position on the afternoon of 7th

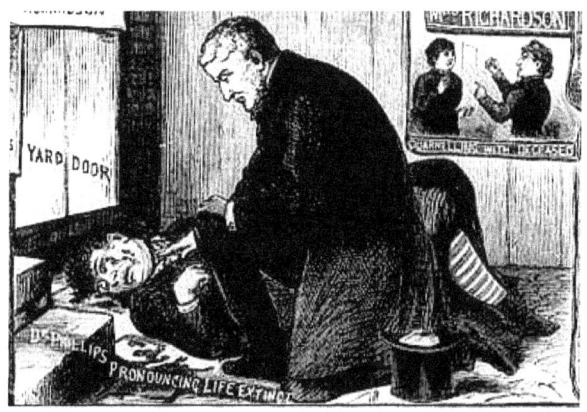

September, when she was about to ejected from Crossingham's as she did not have the necessary money to pay for her bed. Despite being ill, she went out in search of the few pennies needed and met her friend Amelia Palmer on Dorset Street, telling her: "It's no use my giving way. I must pull myself together and go out and get some money, or I shall have no lodgings."

The last definite sighting of Annie Chapman alive was in the early hours of 8th September, when she left Crossingham's for what would be the last time, telling the Deputy "I have not any money now, but don't let the bed; I will be back soon." As she left the lodging house the nightwatchman John Evans saw her enter

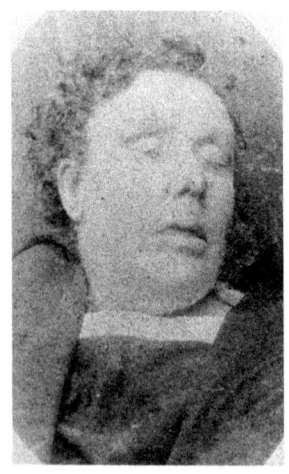

Little Paternoster Row, walking in the direction of Brushfield Street. It was around 1.45am.

At 5.30am Mrs Elizabeth Long was walking along Hanbury Street on her way to Spitalfields Market. As she approached No. 29 she saw a man and woman leaning against the shutters of the house, with the man's back to her. As the woman was facing her, when Mrs Long passed she clearly saw her face, and later identified the body of the victim lying in the mortuary as the same woman – Annie Chapman.

The man appeared to be "a foreigner" over 40 years old, a little taller than the woman. They were talking quite loudly, and Mrs Long heard the man ask "Will you?", and the reply "Yes."

Thirty minutes later Annie's body was found in the rear yard of the house.

ELIZABETH STRIDE

Died 30th September 1888

Described as a quiet woman of mostly sober habits, Elizabeth Stride was a slender 5ft 2in with blue eyes and brown hair, who had been born Elisabeth Gustafsdotter, second child of four to Gustaf Ericsson and his wife Beata at the family's farmhouse at Torslanda, some 16 kilometres from Gothenburg, Sweden, on 27th November 1843.

Finding work as a maidservant for Lars Fredrik Olsson and his family in Majorna, in the suburbs of Gothenburg at almost 18 years of age, Elisabeth found herself without a job when her employment was abruptly terminated after three years in February 1864. She was not yet 21.

Over the course of the following year Elisabeth took maid's jobs around various districts of Gothenburg, but in March 1865, when six months pregnant, she was registered by the Gothenburg police as a prostitute. She was treated for syphilis and as a result went into premature labour, on 21st April delivering a stillborn girl.

After further treatment her fortunes finally took a more positive turn and she found employment with a family who intended travelling to London, and so on 7th February 1866 Elisabeth found herself at the dock

waiting for passage to England.

In time she would meet carpenter John Stride, 13 years her senior, and the couple married in March 1869. They would remain together for a dozen years, in the process moving to Poplar, in the East End, and running a coffee shop for a time, but by December 1881 John and Elizabeth Stride had parted. He died in 1884, while she found a roof over her head first in Brick Lane, and then at her long-time 'home' at 32 Flower and Dean Street.

Elizabeth met waterside labourer Michael Kidney in 1885 and they had been a couple since, although she had left him on a number of occasions; a total of five months over the three years. "It was drink that made her go away, and she always returned without my going after her," Kidney said at her inquest. They lived together on nearby Fashion Street, but according to her friend Catherine Lane, a fellow lodger at 32 Flower and Dean Street, she had "had words" with Kidney and as a result had left.

Those who knew Elizabeth at No. 32 knew she was from Sweden, and some had heard her speak fluently in Swedish to another at the lodging house in addition

to English.

On Saturday, 29th September, the day of her death, she had spent the afternoon cleaning rooms at the lodging house and had earned sixpence from the Deputy, Elizabeth Tanner for her trouble. At eight o'clock that evening she was getting ready to go out. She was wearing a long black coat trimmed with fur and a hat, with a striped coloured handkerchief around her neck. She asked another lodger, barber Charles Preston, if she could borrow his clothes brush. Shortly afterwards she spoke to Mrs Lane, and asked her to look after a piece of velvet until she returned.

She never did.

CATHERINE EDDOWES

Died 30th September 1888

To those around whom she lived her final weeks, the Mitre Square victim was known by the name of Kate

Conway. She had lived with her partner, John Kelly, for seven years at Cooney's Lodging House at 55 Flower and Dean Street – at the other end of the street from Elizabeth Stride – but as the couple had returned to Whitechapel two days earlier – on 28th September – having been hop-picking in Kent as many East Enders did in the summer months, they were penniless that night so both slept at the Casual Ward on Shoe Lane.

The following day John managed to earn 6d through labouring, so while he spent 4d on a bed at Cooney's – the price of a single bed – Kate took the remaining 2d and headed for the Casual Ward at Mile End.

They met the following morning at 8 o'clock and Kate pawned John's boots with Mr Jones at his shop on Church Street, in the shadow of Christ Church, fetching 2s 6d, some of which they spent on supplies of tea and sugar to be kept on her person by Kate and the rest on breakfast, which they ate at Cooney's between 10.00 and 11.00 o'clock.

After their welcome meal the couple found themselves once again without any money, so Kate suggested that she go to Bermondsey, south of the Thames, to see whether she could find her daughter Annie and borrow some. They parted on Houndsditch at 2 o'clock, Kate promising to be back by within a couple of hours. He never saw her alive again.

Later that evening Kelly heard that Kate had been seen with two policemen on Houndsditch, and subsequently locked up at Bishopsgate Police Station because she had had "a drop to drink". Expecting to see her in the morning, he returned to Cooney's alone and took a single bed for the night.

Wherever Kate had spent the afternoon, she had been drinking heavily. It later transpired that her daughter,

Annie Phillips, had moved from Bermondsey some two years earlier, not long after seeing her mother for the last time. She had not left any information as to her new address in order to stop Kate from bothering her for money, which she did often. Whether she even attempted to locate her daughter is unknown; she may well have spent the six hours since parting with John

Kelly still in the East End, for at 8.30pm, not long after Elizabeth Stride had left 32 Flower and Dean Street for the evening, City of London Police officer PC Louis Robinson was on duty in Aldgate High Street when he noticed a number of people gathered around a woman who was lying on the pavement in a drunken slumber; he would later identify her as Kate.

When nobody in the crowd admitted to knowing her, PC Robinson picked Kate up from the floor and tried to get her to stand resting against some shutters, only for her to slide down the wall and back onto the ground. She smelled very strongly of alcohol, and was in such a state that she could not have travelled far before collapsing; she must have been drinking in a nearby pub. With the assistance of another constable, PC Robinson took her to Bishopsgate Police Station, on the way observed by the woman who then informed John Kelly.

On arrival fifteen minutes later she had to be supported by the constables while Station Sergeant James Byfield tried to ascertain her details. When asked her name she gave the reply "Nothing". She was taken to a cell and left there to sleep off her afternoon, being released at one o'clock the following morning to her death.

Taken to the City mortuary at Golden Lane, she was

still officially unidentified. This was soon to change.

When the description was telegraphed around all City stations, PCs Hutt and Simmons both felt this tallied with the drunken woman taken to Bishopsgate on the evening of the 29th; Hutt especially recognised the description of her bonnet, and the fact that she was wearing men's boots. He attended the mortuary and confirmed this was the same woman. The name she had given on her release was 'Mary Ann Kelly', and her address as 6 Fashion Street. These were checked, but obviously drew a blank.

Finally, on the morning of 2nd October, John Kelly walked into Bishopsgate Police Station and said that as a consequence of reading a description of the Mitre Square victim in that morning's newspaper he was convinced that it was his 'wife'. He was convinced because of the two pawn tickets found in possession of the victim, in the names of 'Kelly' and 'Birrell', the latter being a women he and Kate had met when hopping.

He was escorted to the mortuary by Sergeant Miles, and at Golden Lane he confirmed the deceased was his partner of seven years, Kate Conway. Overcome with emotion, back at Bishopsgate Kelly told Major Henry Smith and Superintendent Alfred Foster of his and Kate's movements in the days leading up to her murder, and what he knew of Kate's past. The initials 'T.C.' tattooed on her arm related to her husband Thomas Conway, he informed the officers, but he was uncertain whether Conway was alive or dead. In addition to the daughter he knew Kate had in Bermondsey, there was a sister much closer, in Thrawl Street, Spitalfields.

The sister, Eliza Gold, was soon traced. She also viewed the body at the mortuary and confirmed that it was indeed her sister. Although she had lived for many years with Thomas Conway and they had had children together, Mrs. Gold did not believe they had married; her real name was Catherine Eddowes.

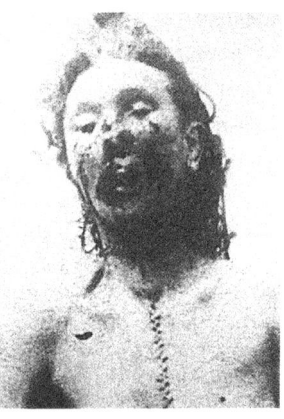

The Midlands girl known as 'Chick' to her family was born on 14th April 1842 at Graiseley Green, near Wolverhampton, to George Eddowes and his wife Catherine Evans. Kate was the sixth of twelve children, half of them born in London following the family's relocation to the capital when she was still a toddler.

Settling in Bermondsey, close to father George's work on the other side of the Thames near London Bridge, Kate was fortunate to receive an education when she was enrolled at the charitable Dowgate School which offered places for the poor of the ward. But the death of both parents by the time Kate was 15-years-old broke up the family; the elder children had in the main formed lives for themselves, while the youngest were admitted to Bermondsey Union Workhouse. 'Chick' was found a position back in Wolverhampton and in

December 1857 went to live with her uncle and aunt, William and Elizabeth Eddowes, and her four young cousins, at their home at 50 Bilston Street.

In the summer of 1862 she met Thomas Conway, a chap-book seller. Quickly falling pregnant, Kate left her life in Wolverhampton behind to join Conway on the road, and the couple travelled around the country. By the time her baby was due Kate found herself in Norfolk, and she gave birth to Catherine Ann 'Annie' Conway at the Great Yarmouth Workhouse infirmary on 18th April 1863. Sons Thomas and George followed in the next decade, but the relationship between Kate and Thomas had already become destructive, through a combination of her drinking and his violent outbursts. They parted in 1881, with Conway taking the children.

Kate gravitated towards the East End and the support of her sister Eliza, who lived at Thrawl Street. Whenever she had the funds, she took a bed at Cooney's Lodging House. It was here that she met John Kelly.

Mrs. Annie Phillips, the daughter Kate told John Kelly that she hoped to see in Bermondsey, had last seen her mother just over two years previously and had subsequently moved to Southwark Park Road. She had never seen any papers, but her mother had told her that she and Thomas Conway had been married. Her father had previously lived with her and her husband, lamp-black packer Louis Phillips, but father and daughter did not get on and he had left suddenly around 18 months ago. She believed he had gone to live with her two brothers, and had not seen him nor heard from him since.

It would take a fortnight for detectives to interview Thomas Conway, and even then it was purely because he had himself attended the City Police's Old Jewry office with his two sons after learning that the police were keen to speak to him. He confirmed his daughter's story, stating that he left Kate in 1880 as a consequence of her drinking. He knew that she had been living with John Kelly, and had seen her once or twice in the streets, but said he kept out of her way as he wanted nothing to do with her.

By the time he attended Old Jewry, his former partner had been in her grave for a week.

MARY KELLY

Died 9th November 1888

Discovering the murder in Miller's Court by virtue of peering through a broken window pane at mounds of bloodied flesh, rent collector Thomas Bowyer and his employer John McCarthy hurriedly walked the short distance to Commercial Street Police Station and there saw Inspector Walter Beck, who listened to their story and immediately followed them back to Miller's Court. The body, John McCarthy told the policeman, was that of Mary Jane Kelly, who together with Joseph Barnett had been his tenant for some ten months. He believed they were married. The rent was 4s 6d a week, but Mary was 29s in arrears, probably as a result of Barnett losing his job as a porter at Billingsgate fish market some three or four months earlier. With no money coming in, Mary had resorted to her old ways by working as a prostitute, although landlord McCarthy claimed that he had no idea his property was being used for immoral purposes.

John McCarthy might have feigned surprise, but the reality is that he must have been aware, and possibly even have expected it. The street had a notorious reputation, as one newspaper described the day after the murder:

"Dorset Street abounds in women whose features, language and behaviour are such that the smallest vestige of self-respect, if any remained in Mary Jane Kelly, would be sufficient to distinguish her from the more degraded of her associates. This short thoroughfare and the adjoining Paternoster Row, leading direct to the Spitalfields vegetable market, have now been given

up to common lodging houses at 4d and 6d a night, or '6d for a single-bedded cabin', and to women who have lost every trace of womanliness. The street and the row are places which the police state are hardly safe for any respectable person by day and certainly not at night. In such a neighbourhood it was impossible to rise; to sink lower was inevitable."

Barnett had left her on 30th October due to her going back to earning a living on the streets. Although he had lost his job at Billingsgate, he found occasional work as a labourer and as a result often visited Mary and gave her money. He went to see her at the Miller's Court room they had previously shared on the evening of 8th November, but as he had not worked that day he had nothing to give her. He departed at 8 o'clock, returning to his new lodgings at Buller's Lodging House on New Street, Bishopsgate.

When he heard the next day that a murder had been committed in Dorset Street he went to the police station, where he was closely questioned and his statement taken. In this way details of Mary Kelly's life were learned; at least, the life as she told it to Joe Barnett.

She was 25-years-old and had been born at Limerick, although her family had moved to Wales when she was very young. Her father's name was John Kelly,

a gauger at an ironworks in Carnarvonshire. She had one sister, who travelled from market to market selling materials, and seven brothers; six at home and one in the army. She had been married at the age of 16 to a collier named Davis or Davies, who had tragically died in an explosion two or three years later.

At that point she had left home and gone to Cardiff, where she lived with a cousin and led "a bad life", before making her way to London and quickly finding work at a brothel in the West End. A man whose acquaintance she met there persuaded her to go to France, and she no doubt went full of excitement at the thought of a life on the Continent. But as she told it to Joe Barnett, Mary did not enjoy the experience and returned to London after a fortnight.

She subsequently lived at various locations including the Ratcliffe Highway, Bethnal Green Road and Pennington Street, sharing her life with men such as a 'Morganstone' and then Joseph Fleming, a plasterer of whom she was apparently fond.

This was her life story before she met Joe Barnett. How much was the truth is impossible to tell, as nothing of her past before her return from Paris has ever been confirmed by researchers.

When the press caught wind that the victim's identity had become known, Joseph Barnett was a wanted man. So many were the inquiries for him at Buller's Lodging House that by the morning following the murder he had been told to leave, his presence "having become a nuisance". Barnett moved in with his sister at 21 Portpool Lane, Grays Inn Road.

He said he had first met Mary Jane Kelly on Commercial Street in April 1887, the two going for a drink and agreeing to meet again the following day, when they decided to remain together. Barnett arranged for a room at George Street, Spitalfields, as he was known there. After a while they moved to Little Paternoster Row, but were told to leave for drunkenness and failing to pay the rent. After living for a short time in Brick Lane, the couple moved to the room which was 13 Miller's Court early in 1888.

On several occasions Mary had asked Barnett to read details of the murders to her; she was apparently afraid, but never named any particular person. The likelihood is that Mary was aware that by earning a living on the streets she was placing herself in danger.

On 9th November when he went to see her a young woman named Lizzie Albrook, who worked at one of the nearby lodging houses, was in the room. Lizzie told reporters of Mary's despair at how working the streets was the only course open to her:

"…She was heartily sick of the life she was leading, and wished she had enough money to go back to her people in Ireland, where her people lived. I don't believe she would have gone out as she did if she had not been obliged to do so in order to keep herself from starvation."

ROSE MYLETT

Died 20th December 1888

In the early hours of 20th December K Division's Sergeant Golding and PC Barrett were on their beat along Poplar High Street when they approached the entrance to Clark's Yard, a large area on the south side of the High Street filled with stables and workshops and accessed via a long, narrow passageway between

Nos. 186 and 188 Poplar High Street.

Sgt Golding looked and saw a bundle some 25 feet into the passage; on examination he discovered it was the body of a woman, lying on its left side with the left cheek resting on the ground. The left arm was under the body, and the left leg drawn up. The clothing was undisturbed. Sgt. Golding touched the body and found it was still warm.

Leaving PC Barrett at the scene, Golding went to fetch Dr Brownfield, K Divisional Surgeon, but finding him unavailable was escorted back to Clark's Yard with his assistant, Dr George Harris. The surgeon examined the body and noted that the lips were livid and the mouth was closed; blood-flecked mucus issued from the nostrils, and the hands were half-clenched. The body was removed to the Bickmore Street mortuary, where Golding searched the clothing and the body was examined.

The body was found to be that of a young woman 5ft 2in tall, with hazel eyes and light-coloured hair which fell in tight curls.

A post mortem was conducted on the still-unknown victim by Dr Brownfield the following morning, and the inquest – presided over by Wynne Baxter was held immediately afterwards. By this time, 24 hours after the discovery of the body, a mark seemingly made by a cord had appeared on the right side of the neck; alongside this were marks obviously caused by thumbs, index and middle fingers on both sides of the neck. Dr Brownfield submitted his opinion that death had been caused by strangulation. Baxter closed proceedings, saying that although it seemed that a murder had been committed there was not yet sufficient evidence. The inquest was adjourned to 2nd January 1889.

Dr Brownfield's comments came as a surprise to

the police, who in the absence of any evidence at the scene had believed the death to have been down to natural causes or suicide. Having read a report of the inquest later that day in an evening newspaper, Assistant Commissioner Robert Anderson suggested to Commissioner James Monro that he should himself go to Poplar to investigate the case, and requested Scotland Yard's Dr Thomas Bond to undertake a second examination alongside Dr Brownfield. The surgeon was unavailable, however, so Chief Surgeon Alexander Mackellar went and made the examination himself. His findings fully supported Dr Brownfield's opinion that death was by strangulation. Dr Bond and his assistant Dr Hebbert later viewed the body and concurred with the earlier findings. Anderson was certain that the case was not one of murder, and on 24th December Dr Bond made another examination and reported to Anderson that he had changed his mind; death *was* due to strangulation, but accidental and not murder.

She would soon be identified; her name was Catherine Mylett, known sometimes as 'Rose', and her mother lived in Pelham Street, near Baker's Row in Whitechapel. A newspaper report of police officers arriving at the house to break the news gives a sad insight into the reaction of those personally affected by this series of murders:

"When the detectives called at the house on Boxing Day they found the inmates indulging in Christmas festivities, and upon stating the object of their visit one of the women in the house had a serious fit."

Investigations were undertaken by Chief Inspector Donald Swanson of Scotland Yard and K Division's Inspector Richard Wildey, and their efforts were soon rewarded, when they visited Charles Ptolomey, the Night Attendant at the Poplar Union:

"They asked me if I could identify the sailors? I told them I could pick the men out of a thousand. How I came to notice them was in this way: It was about five minutes to eight o'clock on Wednesday night, when I was going to my work. Upon going up England Row (nearly opposite Clark's yard) I noticed two sailors. The shorter one was speaking to the deceased, and the tall one was walking up and down. So strange did it seem that I stopped and 'took account' of them. Then I heard the woman say several times "No; no! no!" and the short sailor spoke in a low tone. The tall one was about 5ft 11in. He looked like a Yankee. The shorter one was about 5ft 7in. It struck me that they were there for no good purpose, and that was the reason I took so much notice of their movements. I shall always remember their faces, and could, as I say, pick them out of a thousand. I have been to the mortuary, and seen the deceased. She is the same woman, and she was sober when I saw her with the sailors."

Despite conflicting medical evidence, at the conclusion of the inquest the jury returned a verdict of 'Wilful murder against some person or persons unknown'.

In his summing up Coroner Wynne Baxter was afforded the opportunity to vent his frustration at how the Metropolitan Police had sought the opinion of a number of medical men, seemingly in an attempt to prove that the death did not belong in the same class as the previous murders in Whitechapel.

Clinging obstinately to his view that Catherine Mylett had died from natural causes, Assistant Commissioner Robert Anderson would later write that "but for the 'Jack the Ripper' scare, no one would have thought of suggesting that it was a homicide."

ALICE MCKENZIE

Died 17th July 1889

On Monday, 16th July labourer John McCormack arrived back at his lodgings at 52 Gun Street, Spitalfields from his job at a Jewish tailors on Hanbury Street. It was four o'clock, and after giving some money to his common-law wife Alice McKenzie he retired to bed for a few hours. The couple had been together for seven years, living in various lodging houses around Spitalfields but for the past year had been at Gun Street, which was nicknamed 'Tenpenny's' after the owner, Mr Thomas Tempany.

Before meeting John McCormack, Alice McKenzie had lived for some time with a blind man who made a living playing a concertina in the streets, but he had died around 1878. McCormack would later say that as far as he knew Alice had no relatives in London, but

believed she had one son who was in America. Both her parents were dead, but she often spoke about her father, who had been a postman in Peterborough, and McCormack believed that's where Alice originated from.

She was described as around 40 years of age, a freckle-faced woman who was more often than not seen puffing on a pipe, earning her the nickname 'Clay Pipe' Alice.

When McCormack woke around 11.00 o'clock Alice had gone out. Deputy Betsy Ryder had seen her walk through the kitchen and out the front door onto Gun Street at around 8.30pm.

The next definite sighting of Alice McKenzie alive came at 11.40pm. Margaret Franklin, who had known her for 14 or 15 years, was sitting with two friends on the step of a barber's shop at the Brick Lane end of Flower and Dean Street when she walked past, heading in the direction of Whitechapel. She paused briefly to talk but said she couldn't stop, then continued on her way.

At 12.20am, 40 minutes later, PC Walter Andrews was walking his beat and passed through Castle Alley, which ran parallel to Goulston Street. He saw nothing to attract his attention. At 12.30am PC Allen entered the street and stopped for five minutes under the lamp outside the offices of Messrs. David S. King and Sons to enjoy some supper. He too noticed nothing suspicious, and on finishing his food went back to his duty. At 12.48am PC Andrews returned to Castle Alley on another circuit, when Sergeant Badham approached on his check of the patrols. On receiving the "Alright" he left Andrews, but had gone no further than 150 yards when he heard the shrill blast of the constable's whistle. He rushed back to Castle Alley and found PC Andrews standing over the body of a woman, a pool of blood around her head and her skirts pushed up to expose her abdomen. She was lying under the very lamp at which PC Allen had enjoyed his supper.

Allen was alerted by Sgt. Badham and went to fetch Dr Bagster Phillips; PC Andrews remained with the body. He touched the body, and felt that it was quite warm.

Dr Phillips arrived at 1.10am and conducted an examination; the victim was lying on her back, with her face turned to the right. Her eyelids were open, her pupils dilated. There were two deep wounds in the left side of the neck from which a large amount of blood had flowed into the gutter.

The body was removed to the mortuary and at two o'clock that same afternoon Dr Phillips conducted a post mortem on the body, who had by now been identified by Mrs Ryder as being that of Alice McKenzie. Doctors Gordon Brown and Mackellar were in attendance as Phillips carried out his work. Death had been caused by the wounds to the throat, and seven or eight superficial wounds on the stomach and pubic area indicated an attempt at mutilation.

Wynne Baxter presided over the inquest, which opened at five o'clock that day and concluded on 14th August 1889. It returned a verdict of 'Murder against a person or persons unknown'. Alice McKenzie had by this time been buried at the East London Cemetery on 24th July, a quiet affair attended by only a handful of her friends.

Interestingly, Assistant Commissioner Robert Anderson had asked Dr Thomas Bond to conduct his own examination, which he did assisted by Dr Bagster Phillips on 18th July, the day after the murder. Anderson was obviously keen for Scotland Yard's medico-legal expert to compare the murder of Alice McKenzie with the 1888 crimes, and the doctor did not disappoint, writing:

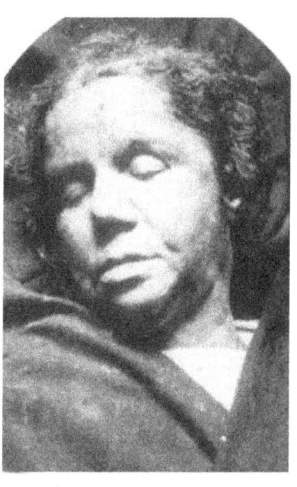

"I see in this murder evidence of similar design to the former Whitechapel murders viz. sudden onslaught on the prostrate woman, the throat skilfully & resolutely cut with subsequent mutilation, each mutilation indicating sexual thoughts & a desire to mutilate the abdomen & sexual organs. I am of the opinion that the murder was performed by the same person who committed the former series of Whitechapel murders."

Given that Thomas Bond's report profiling the murderer in November 1888 has shaped the way we think about the victims in the series of Ripper killings, it seems probable that, had Robert Anderson asked him to write his profile following the murder of Alice McKenzie, we would now, all these years later, be debating a Canonical Six.

THE PINCHIN STREET TORSO

Died circa 9th September 1889

Unsurprisingly, given the victim in this sickening case was never identified, very little is known about the women who was so horribly mutilated and unceremoniously dumped in a railway arch.

In the early hours of 10th September 1889 the body of a woman minus the head and legs was discovered by PC William Pennett as he walked his beat along Pinchin Street, a quiet road alongside railway arches a few minutes south of Berner Street. There was no blood within the arch in which the trunk was discovered, indicating that the victim had been killed elsewhere and dismemberment – whether death had been through murder or not – hadn't taken place where the body was found.

Medical examination suggested that death had occurred at least twenty-four hours before the discovery, so the trunk must have been kept in some place for a day or two before a decision was made where to dispose of it.

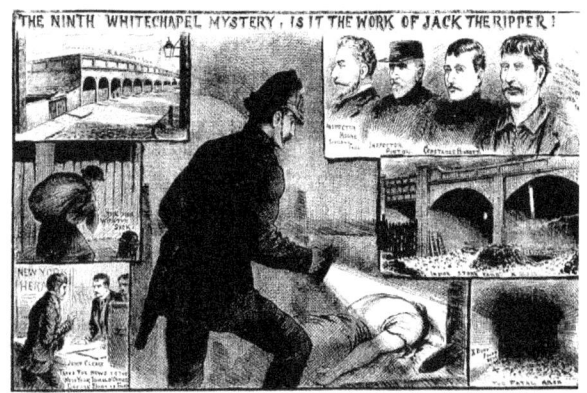

From the size of the torso and arm length, it was estimated that the victim had been "a woman of stoutish build, dark complexion, about 5ft 3in in height, and between 30 and 40 years of age."

The police seemed to be presented with a lead when the next day's *New York Herald* published a story claiming that a man had called at their offices with information about a murder supposedly committed in Backchurch Lane, which terminated at its southern end into Pinchin Street.

The story claimed that the informant, John Cleary, revealed to reporters that he had been told about a terrible murder and mutilation by an acquaintance, who happened to be an inspector of police. The two journalists rushed to a cab in order to visit the scene, but Cleary refused to join them. On arrival they walked the length of Backchurch Lane and the surrounding area, but all was quiet. They reportedly met two police officers who knew nothing of the supposed murder, so the reporters returned to their office.

The rumoured murder might otherwise have been forgotten had it not been for the discovery of the trunk in Pinchin Street two days later; Dr George Bagster Phillip's assistant Percy Clark had estimated death to have occurred 48 hours before discovery. Had the murder taken place as claimed by the informant?

The torso was buried in a sealed metal box filled with spirits, designed to preserve the flesh for matching with the legs and head should they be discovered, and lies silently waiting for such an identification to this day.

FRANCES COLES

Died 13th February 1891

At 2.15am on 13th February 1891 PC Ernest Thompson, who had only joined the Met three months earlier, was walking his first solo beat along Chamber Street when he heard the sound of a man's footsteps retreating. Seconds later he was at Swallow Gardens and, turning on his lamp, discovered Frances

Coles lying on the ground, surrounded by a pool of blood. Despite her throat having been cut she was still alive – just – and as PC Thompson looked he saw the faint movement of one eyelid.

As Police Orders dictated an officer remain with a victim should they be alive, Thompson was unable to pursue the footsteps and the probable killer of Frances Coles – and possibly Jack the Ripper. She soon died from her wounds.

The victim was known to police as a prostitute; she was in her mid-20s, 5ft tall with dark brown hair and eyes. On the night of her death she was wearing old, dark clothes.

She had been born in Bermondsey in September 1859 to bootmaker James Cole and his wife Mary Ann Carney. By 1880 Frances had found a job 'stoppering bottles' for a wholesale chemist shop in the Minories, a job she told older sister Mary Ann was painful to her knuckles, and she apparently left the position at some point in the early 1880s.

Despite subsequently earning a living walking the streets for some years, Frances did her best to keep this a secret from her family, telling them she continued to work at the chemists and was living with an elderly woman in Richard Street, Commercial Road.

Following the discovery of her body, the archway

of Swallow Gardens was quickly filled with police officers and medical men, closed to the public. H Division's Superintendent Arnold and Inspector Reid were joined shortly before 5.00am by Chief Inspector Swanson from Scotland Yard, and the detectives under their command carried out a thorough examination of the area. In a space between a waterpipe and some brickwork two shillings wrapped in a sheet of newspaper were discovered; whether these had been put there by the victim was impossible to prove. With their investigations completed, and the body removed to the mortuary, Swanson ordered that a small amount of the blood on the ground be collected for analysis and the rest washed away. The archway was then opened to traffic.

The victim had spent two days drinking with a ship's fireman named James Thomas Sadler, who had been discharged from SS *Fez* as she berthed in the East End docks and made his way the short distance to Whitechapel to begin spending his pay. He met Frances Coles, of whom he had been a former client, at the Princess Alice, and she certainly helped with his spending, the pair touring the pubs of Spitalfields and Whitechapel over the next couple of days.

Late in the evening of 12th February Coles and Sadler had a drunken argument after she refused to

go to his aid when he was attacked and robbed, and as a result went their separate ways.

Frances returned to their lodgings at Spitalfields Chambers. She sat at a bench in the kitchen and fell asleep with her head on her arms. Sadler also soon returned, face bloodied and bruised, but after bathing his wounds was forced to leave as he had no money. When Frances woke up she was also ejected.

At 1.30am she bumped into fellow prostitute Ellen Callana by the Princess Alice on Commercial Street. As they walked together in the direction of the Minories,

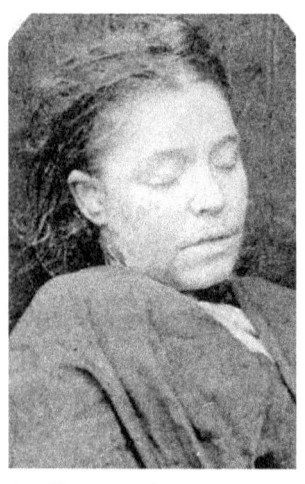
"a very short man with a dark moustache, shiny boots and blue trousers" approached Callana and solicited her; she refused his offer, at which the man punched her in the face and tore her jacket. He then walked over to Frances who, ignoring her friend's warning, walked away with the stranger in the direction of the Minories and Swallow Gardens.

Around the same time Sadler had made his way to St Katherine Dock and attempted to force his way onto the SS *Fez*, despite being discharged two days earlier. For his troubles he got into another fight, this time with dockworkers, which left him with a wound to his head. He wandered around Whitechapel until the early hours, when he at last gave in to his injuries and a constable on duty in Whitechapel Road helped him to the London Hospital across the road to seek medical attention.

When the body of Frances Coles was discovered

Sadler found himself in trouble; he had been seen in her company for a prolonged period of time and was the obvious suspect for her murder. Around midday on the 14th he was apprehended by Sergeant John Don of R Division and, escorted by H Division's PC Gill, taken to Leman Street Police Station, where Chief Inspector Swanson was waiting. The detective took a statement, with Sadler appearing to be completely open. Given the number of public houses mentioned, it was a surprise that he would recall any events of his time with Frances.

With a likely murder suspect in custody for the first time, the police stepped up efforts to link Sadler with the atrocities of 1888. It was reported that they had confronted one of the three men who had seen Catherine Eddowes at the entrance to Church Passage with the prisoner, but the attempted identification proved unsuccessful.

At the inquest into Coles' death, evidence was heard that Sadler was so drunk by the time of her murder that it was extremely unlikely that he would have been capable of the deed, a fact commented on by Coroner Wynne Baxter in his summing up. On 27th February the jury returned a verdict of 'Willful Murder against some person or persons unknown', and, thanks to legal representation paid for by the Seamen's Union, at a hearing at Thames Magistrates' Court four days later all charges were dropped against him. As he left the court, crowds of people cheered his release.

The press were straightforward in their opinion:

NOT "JACK THE RIPPER"

"The unkempt fireman Sadler, who was arrested for the murder of Frances Coles, has disappointed the London police who hoped he would turn out to be the mysterious fiend responsible for the Whitechapel horrors. There is nothing for it but for the police to begin de novo, and it is, no doubt, heartbreaking work to be foiled time after time, and to feel powerless to mend matters."

Although they didn't know it at the time, the murder of Frances Coles would be the last to be added to the Whitechapel file.

VISITING THE GRAVES OF THE WHITECHAPEL VICTIMS

Paying one's respects at the gravesides of the victims named in the Whitechapel murders case file is not as straightforward as one would like. Sadly, the final resting places of Emma Smith and Martha Tabram have been lost to time, although they are almost certainly buried in one of the East London cemeteries. As the murders of first Polly Nichols and then Annie Chapman thrust the series into the national spotlight, their funerals and those following were reported in detail, and we are therefore able to visit markers dedicated to their memory.

However, the grave sites of all the Whitechapel murder victims have long since been re-used and renumbered, and now only the canonical five are commemorated, two having graves and three having memorial plaques in their name.

Mary Ann Nichols and **Catherine Eddowes** are both buried in the City of London Cemetery, Manor Park (Aldersbrook Road, E12 5DQ. Mon-Fri 9.00am-6.30pm, weekends 9.00am-4.30pm), while **Annie**

Chapman lies in Manor Park Cemetery (Sebert Road, E7 0NP. Mon-Fri 9.00am-4.30pm, weekends 10.00am-3.30pm). **Mary Kelly** is buried in St Patrick's Roman Catholic Cemetery (Langthorne Road, E11 4HL. Mon-Fri 8.00am-4.00pm, weekends 9.00am-5.00pm). **Elizabeth Stride**'s grave is in the East London Cemetery (Grange Road E13 0HB. Mon-Fri 8.30am-4.30pm, weekends 9.30am-4.30pm), as are the remains of **Alice McKenzie**, **Frances Coles** and the woman whose torso was found in **Pinchin Street**.

Although the graves can be visited in isolation, if you're planning on making a journey to all on the same day I recommend starting at the City of London Cemetery, which is best reached from central London by taking an overground train from Liverpool Street Station to Manor Park Station, a thirteen minute journey.

The journey described over the following pages takes in all the cemeteries mentioned above and the public transport which links them. A Day Travelcard allows you travel on all rail, tube and buses used in this trip.

On arrival at Manor Park Station, exit the station and turn left along Forest Drive, over Whitta Road, and continue along with Manor Park on your right. Continue ahead over Capel Road, and just keep

Edgar's Guide To...

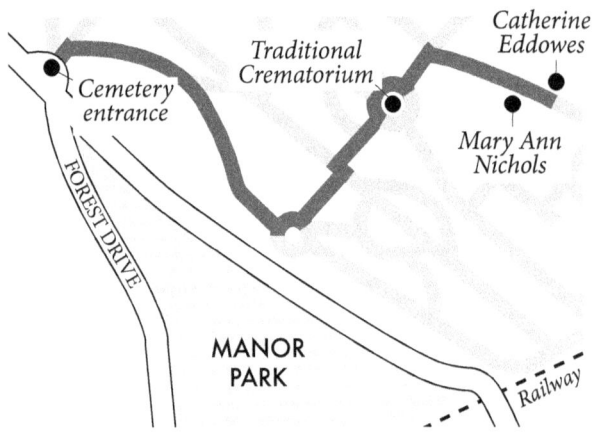

walking until you reach the roundabout, on the other side of which you will see the stone gateway of the City of London Cemetery. Cross over to it and enter the cemetery via the main gate.

☞ DIRECTIONS TO THE MEMORIAL PLAQUES

Just past two black bollards on the right, turn right and begin walking along that path – you will see a sign and an arrow pointing to 'Traditional Crematorium' and 'Memorial Gardens' on the left side of the path. Keep ahead along the path, and at the crossroads turn right (the white cross on the grave of George Leslie Drewry will be to your right on the corner as you turn right). Keep ahead along that asphalt roadway, and in a little while, away to your left, you will see the red-tiled roof of the Traditional Crematorium. This is what you will be heading for, so look out for the left turn towards it – just after a red circled '10' speed limit sign – then walk to the Crematorium, proceed clockwise around it, and then continue straight along the path on its other side. You will pass a pond on your right, and then turn right along Memorial Gardens, Gardens Way and keep ahead, to pass the end of a hedge on your right, and, a little further along, you will pass the end of a wall, and a line of trees. A little way along, flat on the grass on the right, you will find the memorial plaque to Mary Ann Nichols.

....

MARY ANN NICHOLS

It is generally accepted that Mary Ann 'Polly' Nichols was the first victim of Jack the Ripper. She was murdered in Buck's Row on 31st August 1888.

Her funeral took place on 6th September 1888, and a report about it appeared in the next day's *South Wales Echo*:

"*The funeral of Mary Ann Nichols, who was murdered in Buck's Row, early on Friday morning, took place yesterday.*

The time at which the cortège was to start was kept secret, and a ruse was resorted to in order to get the body out of the mortuary, where it has lain since the day of the murder.

A pair-horsed closed hearse was observed making its way down Hanbury Street, and the crowds, which numbered some thousands, made way for it to go along Old Montague Street; but instead of so doing it passed on into Whitechapel Road, and doubling back it reached the mortuary by the back gate, which is situated in Chapman's Court.

No person was near, other than the undertaker and his men, when the coffin, which bore a plate with the inscription, 'Mary Ann Nichols, aged 42. Died August 31, 1888', was removed to the hearse and driven off to Hanbury Street, there to await the mourners. Meantime the news had spread that the body was in the hearse, and people flocked round to see the coffin. At length the cortège started towards Ilford.

The mourners were Mr Edward Walker, the father of the deceased, and his grandson, together with two of the deceased's children.

The procession proceeded along Baker's Row, and past

the corner of Buck's Row, into the main road, where policemen were stationed every few yards. The houses in the neighbourhood had the blinds drawn, and much sympathy was expressed for the relatives."

☞ *Keep going along the path; you will pass a white information board on your left, and, a little further along, again flat on the grass, this time on the left side of the path, you will find the memorial plaque to Catherine Eddowes.*

CATHERINE EDDOWES

Generally considered to have been the fourth victim of Jack the Ripper, Catherine was murdered in Mitre Square on 30th September 1888. Her funeral took place on the afternoon of Monday, 8th October 1888. That evening the *Nottingham Evening Post* carried a brief report on the events of the day:

"The funeral of Catherine Eddowes, the victim of the Mitre Square murder, took place this afternoon at Ilford, Essex, where the City of London Cemetery is situated. The expenses of the funeral were borne entirely by a private citizen.

The corpse, decently laid in a plain coffin, with the name and age of deceased engraved thereon, was removed at half-past one from the Golden Lane Mortuary.

Thousands of people lined the streets in the vicinity of the cemetery, evincing much sympathy. The remains were borne in an open hearse, followed by two carriage. Several wreaths were on the coffin.

The crowds in the streets of the East End were so dense that a force of police had to direct the traffic."

The following weekend, the *Warminster and Westbury Journal, and Wilts County Advertiser*, carried a report about the funeral in its edition of Saturday, 13th October 1888, which went into more detail about the behaviour of the crowd:

"The funeral of Catherine Eddowes, the victim of the Mitre Square murder, took place on Monday afternoon. The body was removed from the City mortuary in Golden Lane at a quarter past one o'clock for interment in the City of London cemetery, at Ilford. There were dense crowds in the vicinity of Golden Lane, and at the junctions of Osborn and Commercial Streets the people were so numerous that a large force of police had to direct the traffic. The body was conveyed in an open hearse, a wreath being placed on either side of the coffin. Following the remains were two mourning coaches, and in the rear of these was a large waggon crowded with

women, the majority of whom were attired in a style not at all befitting the occasion."

Once you have viewed the two memorial plaques, you can backtrack to the main gate to exit the cemetery, then make your way to Manor Park Cemetery.

☞ *Retrace your footsteps to Manor Park Station, turning right along Whitta Road just before it. At the end of the road you will come to the gates of Manor Park Cemetery. Enter the Cemetery, and, a very short distance along the path, you will see two trees on the left. Go along the grass path that starts to the left of these two trees and, as the modern graves give way to an older area of graves on the left, you will see the memorial plaque to Annie Chapman.*

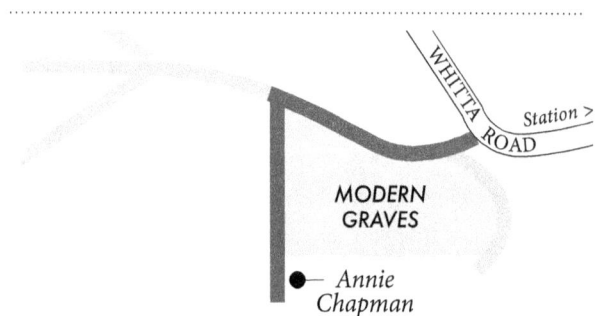

ANNIE CHAPMAN

Believed to have been the second victim of Jack the Ripper, Annie was buried on 14th September 1888. *The People* of 16th September gave the following account of the funeral:

"The funeral of Annie Chapman, the last victim of the Whitechapel murderer, took place early on Friday morning. The utmost secrecy was observed in the arrangements, and none but the undertaker, the police and the relatives of the deceased knew anything about it. Shortly after seven o'clock a hearse drew up outside the mortuary in Montague Street, and the body was quickly removed. At nine o'clock a start was made for Manor

Park Cemetery, the place selected by the friends of the deceased for the interment, but no coaches followed, as it was desired that public attention should not be attracted. Mr Smith and other relatives met the body at the cemetery, and the service was duly performed in the ordinary manner. The remains of the deceased were enclosed in a black covered elm coffin, which bore the words, 'Annie Chapman, died September the 8th, 1888, aged 48 years.'"

....

To visit the grave of Mary Kelly, we must visit St Patrick's Roman Catholic Cemetery in Leytonstone. Backtrack along Whitta Road, go right at its end, and keep ahead past Manor Park Station. You will come to a bus stop, on the same side as the station and outside the Blakesley Arms, from which you will need to take bus 101 to Wanstead Underground Station (approximately a 20 minute bus ride). The nearest stop is opposite George Green, and is designated stop B. On alighting from the bus turn right, and Wanstead Underground Station is situated on the right side of the main road, just beyond the traffic lights. From here you can take the Central Line to Leyton Underground Station, a five minute journey. On arrival, exit Leyton Station and turn left along Leyton High Road. In a few moments, past the tall controlled zone sign on your left, turn left down the steps which will bring you down onto Goodall Road. Turn left and follow Goodall Road to its end, then turn right into what is now Elmore Road, walking with a metal fence on your left. Follow the road round to the left, where it becomes Langthorne Road, and shortly you will see the gates to St Patrick's Roman Catholic Cemetery on your left. Go in through the cemetery gates and keep ahead, passing to the left of the chapel building. Pause by the two white posts on the left and, to their left, you will see the grave of the McCarthy family, marked by a large memorial with a large standing angel on top of it. Amongst those buried here is John McCarthy, who was Mary Kelly's landlord.

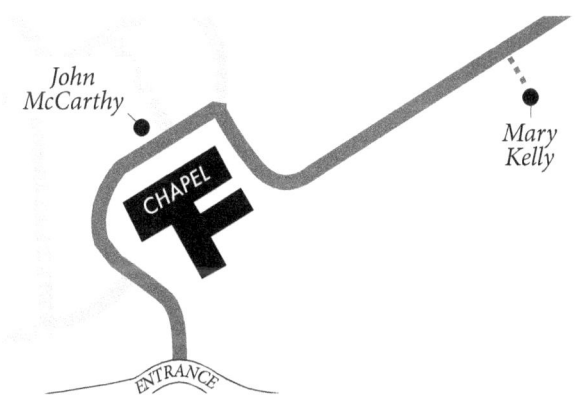

Continue past the McCarthy family grave and follow the path as it bends right, and then turn left along the path, just after the tree. When you reach a waste bin on the right, built from pale green stone blocks, look ahead and right past a stone cross and you will see a white statue of a footballer. To the right of this, you will find the grave of Mary Kelly.

You will see that, despite the fact that the inscription appears to be somewhat worn away, people regularly come here and leave flowers to her memory. The inscription on it reads: "In Loving Memory of Marie Jeanette Kelly", followed by the poignant lines"

> *"None But The Lonely Hearts*
> *Can Know My Sadness,*
> *Love Lives Forever."*

MARY KELLY

The funeral of Mary Kelly on 19th November 1888 was an emotion-charged affair, and was reported as follows in *Lloyd's Weekly Newspaper* of 25th November 1888:

"The funeral of Marie Jeanette Kelly took place at Leytonstone cemetery in the presence of large number of people. An hour before the remains left the mortuary many hundreds of persons assembled around

Shoreditch church, and watched in silence the funeral arrangements. On the coffin were placed two crowns and a cross, made of heartsease and white flowers. The cross had been subscribed for by the murdered woman's associates in Dorset Street. Attached to it was a large card, bearing the words, "A last tribute of respect to Mary Kelly. May she rest in peace, and may her murderer be brought to justice." The whole the funeral expenses were defrayed by Mr. Wilton, who for 50 years has acted as sexton to St. Leonard's, Shoreditch, in the mortuary of which the body has been lying. At half-past 12 the coffin was borne from the mortuary,

and the cemetery at Leytonstone was reached at two o'clock. The Rev. Father Columban, with two acolytes, and a cross bearer, met the body at the door of the little chapel, of St. Patrick, and the coffin was carried at once to a grave in the north-western corner. Barnett and the poor women who had accompanied the funeral knelt on the cold clay by the side of the grave, while the service was read by Father Columban. The coffin was incensed, lowered, and then sprinkled with holy water, and the simple ceremony ended. The floral ornaments were afterwards raised to be placed upon the grave, and the filling-up was completed in a few moments, and was watched by a small crowd of people."

....

Once you have paid your visit to Mary Kelly's grave, retrace your footsteps back to Leyton Station and, as you climb the steps from Goodall Road head left to the bus stop designated A and take a 69 bus to the East London Cemetery, the stop being diagonally opposite the cemetery gates. Buses on this route are very regular, and the journey time between the two cemeteries is approximately 30 minutes.

Once inside the gates of the East London Cemetery, keep straight ahead towards the Celtic cross war memorial. On arrival at the memorial turn left along the path and keep ahead, following the main path as it

Jack the Ripper's East End

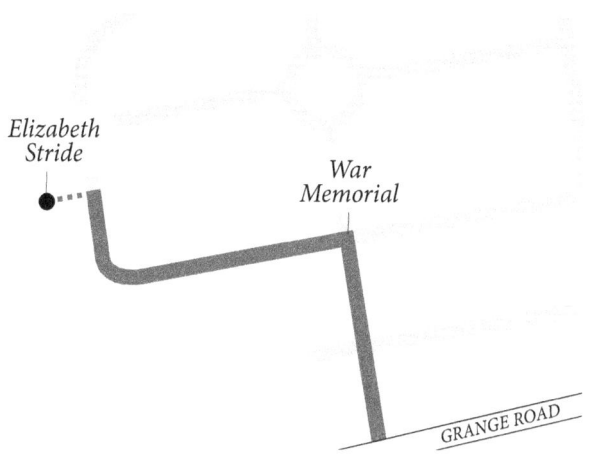

swings round to the right. Keep ahead along that path, passing a grey waste bin on the left.

Just after you have passed a second waste bin on the left, bear left along a gravel path and, a little way along on the left side, you will arrive at the grave of Elizabeth Stride.

ELIZABETH STRIDE

In contrast to the relative grandeur of some of her fellow victims, Elizabeth was buried with the minimum of fuss at the East London Cemetery on 6th October at the expense of the parish.

The *Glasgow Herald* of 8th October 1888 reported on a strange incident which had taken place on the evening of the funeral. Elizabeth's spirit had apparently been summoned by a group of six people at Cardiff, one of whom – a respectable-looking elderly lady who identified herself as a spiritualist – attended the local police station to report that Elizabeth had told them that her murderer was a middle-aged man who lived on Commercial Street or Road. She apparently mentioned his name, and the fact that he was one of a gang of twelve.

Also resting within the grounds of East London Cemetery, but without a grave or even a formal marker, lie the bodies of Alice McKenzie, Frances Coles and the woman sadly known for posterity as 'the Pinchin Street torso'.

Alice McKenzie was laid to rest here on 24th July 1889, and that day's *Nottingham Evening Post* reported her funeral as follows:

"The funeral of Alice McKenzie, the latest victim of the Whitechapel murderer, took place this afternoon at Plaistow Cemetery. Many of the inhabitants of the neighbourhood in which the murder was committed assembled outside the public-house to which the remains were brought from the mortuary at half-past one. There was no excitement. The coffin was placed in an open hearse, and followed by two mourning coaches

containing three or four friends of the deceased. The funeral expenses were defrayed by local subscription."

A much grander affair was held for the interment of **Francis Coles** on 25th February 1891. The following day, a reporter from *The Echo* related the occasion:

"The funeral of Frances Coles, the victim of the last Whitechapel murder, was yesterday made the occasion of the gathering of vast crowds in the East End and in the East London Cemetery, where the interment took place. It was noted as a curious circumstance that whereas the population of the eastern portions of the Metropolis have displayed scarcely any concern in the proceedings

connected with the investigation of the crime committed in their midst at Swallow Gardens, on the 13th inst., the liveliest interest was manifested in the burial of the deceased. On Monday, when it was originally intended that the ceremony should take place, nearly 15,000 people flocked to Plaistow only to be disappointed.

Yesterday afternoon the brilliant sunshine and springlike weather, which succeeded the dispersal of the fog, induced a much larger number of persons to journey to the graveside, whilst all along the five or six miles of route, from Whitechapel to beyond Canning Town, the streets were lined with spectators. Naturally the mob was thickest and most typical of the locality upon Mile End "Waste," where factory girls, boys, and men and women inhabiting the congested streets branching from the main roads, congregated during the dinner hour, waiting for the arrival of the mourning coaches from the City, and the appearance of the hearse from the yard attached to the Whitechapel mortuary. A brisk trade was done in "In Memoriam" cards, and the kerbstone vocalists invited patronage by their rendering of the latest patriotic songs of the day. Chief Inspector West was on the scene with a large staff of police at his command.

The funeral arrangements had been entrusted by the father of the deceased to the London Common Lodging-

House Mission, and it was from the offices of this society in Ludgate Circus that three carriages started. The first contained Mr Coles, the father, and Miss Mary Ann Coles, the sister, of the murdered woman; Mr A.H. Shepherd, one of the vice-presidents of the mission; Mr John Harvey, the hon. secretary; and the Rev D. Thomas, of Grove Road, Victoria Park. In the second were Mrs Harvey, Mrs Bordman, and Mrs Day, representing the lady workers of the mission; and in the third Mr F.C. Paynter, honorary solicitor; Mr Maysmith, and Mr Johnson.

About five hundred people marched on each side of the hearse, which fully exposed the polished elm and white-metal mounted coffin to view. The plate was simply inscribed with the name of the deceased, the date of her death, and her age (26). A few wreaths were placed about it, one of them having been sent from Maidstone.

The route to the cemetery, after leaving the Mile End Road, was by way of Burdett Road, into the East India Dock Road, at the junction of which large numbers of people were collected, and thence across the iron bridge to Barking Road, the time occupied in traversing this distance being nearly an hour and a-half.

In the cemetery fully 20,000 people had assembled, and the majority of these, when it was noticed that the hearse was taking a lower road through the grounds, made a wild stampede across the grass, tumbling down in their haste, shrieking and laughing in the most unseemly manner. Mr Murray, superintendent of the cemetery, had, however, made effectual arrangements to ensure the utmost decorum in the immediate vicinity of the grave. A securely roped-off enclosure marked the spot, and half-a-dozen policemen kept the crowd from encroaching upon its limits.

The site assigned to the last resting-place of Frances Coles is within a few yards of the graves of Mary Ann Nichols [sic], Annie Chapman [sic], Elizabeth Stride, and Mary Jane Kelly [sic], four of the women murdered in Whitechapel and Spitalfields during the year 1888; and close by lie buried the mutilated remains of the unknown woman whose dismembered body was discovered in Pinchin Street in the autumn of 1889.

The burial service was short and simple, being conducted by the Rev D. Thomas, who, in his prayer, supplicated the Almighty "to bring to the bar of justice the cruel hand that smote the death blow, so that right might be done," and "that which cried from the very ground for vengeance might be heard and answered."

There were addressed delivered at the graveside by Mr Thomas, Mr Harvey, and Mr Paynter, the last gentleman remarking that Mr Coles had assured him that his daughter had never given him any trouble or pain during her life. The father, who appeared in a feeble state, and shed tears abundantly, took a last look at the coffin, and was then led away to the carriage in waiting. Happily he did not see the crowd surge over the ropes and nearly throw the two attendant policemen into the open grave."

Somewhere within these grounds also lies the unique coffin containing the remains of the woman who was found dismembered in **Pinchin Street**, buried on 5th October 1889 in a metal box filled with spirits to preserve the torso should the missing body parts be discovered.

The cemetery itself is a pleasant enough spot in which to while away an hour or so once you have visited Liz Stride's grave, and there are a number of benches just along from her final resting place where you can sit and reflect on the fate of all the victims laid to rest here. There are also public toilets in the waiting area around the central chapel.

GETTING BACK TO LONDON

Exit the cemetery via the main gates and turn left along Grange Road. After a few minutes' walk along here you will come to a bus stop, from which you can take the 69 bus to Stratford Station, a twenty minute journey. Once at Stratford you can then take the Underground (Central Line) or mainline rail back to central London.

www.ingramcontent.com/pod-product-compliance
Lightning Source LLC
Chambersburg PA
CBHW051125160426
43195CB00014B/2354